MASQUERADE

coloring ◆ expression ◆ book

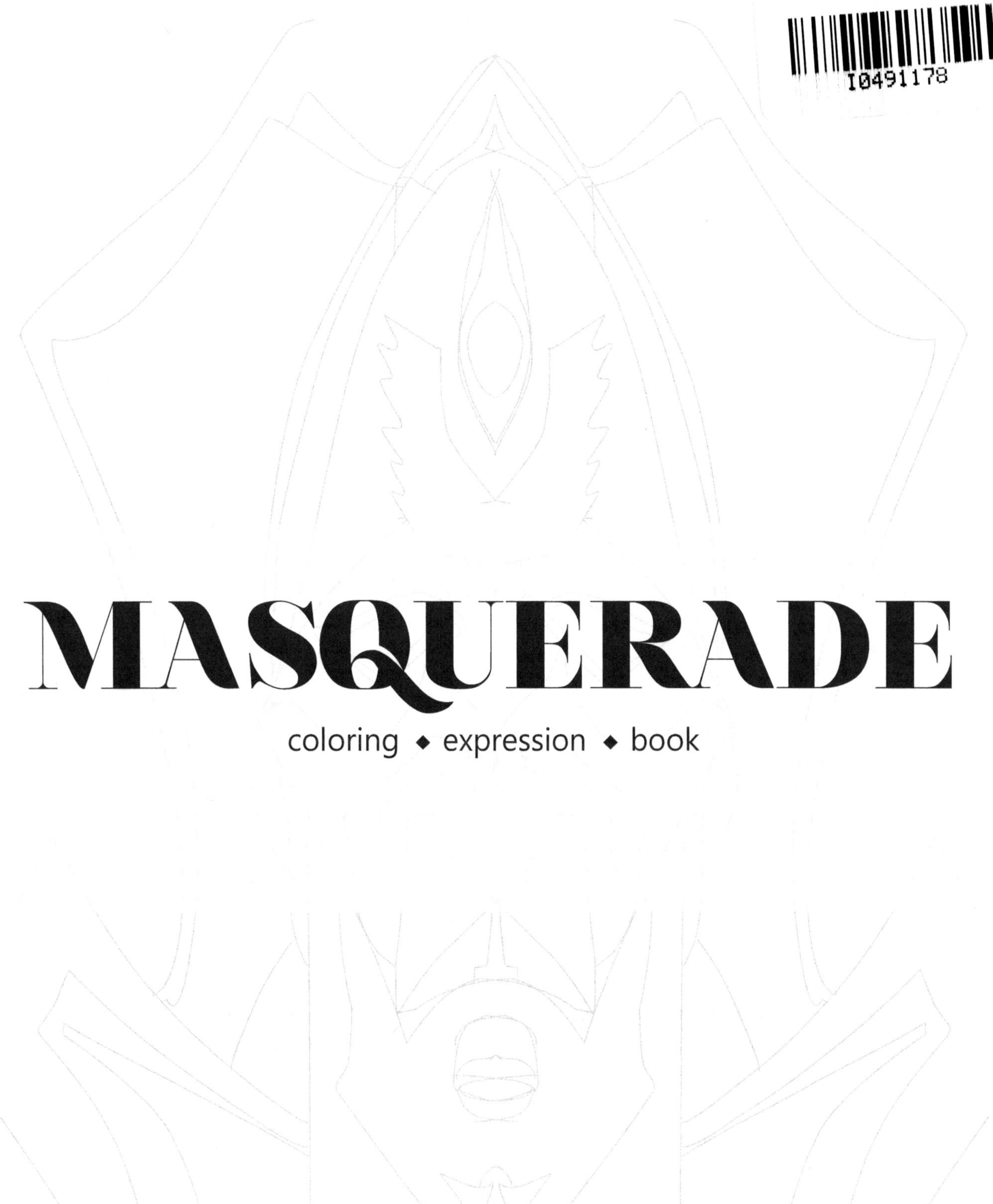

Published by Gaddier Fine Art Studio
Illustrations and cover art by Gaddier Rosario

ISBN: 9798682244331

GADDIER

FINE ART STUDIO

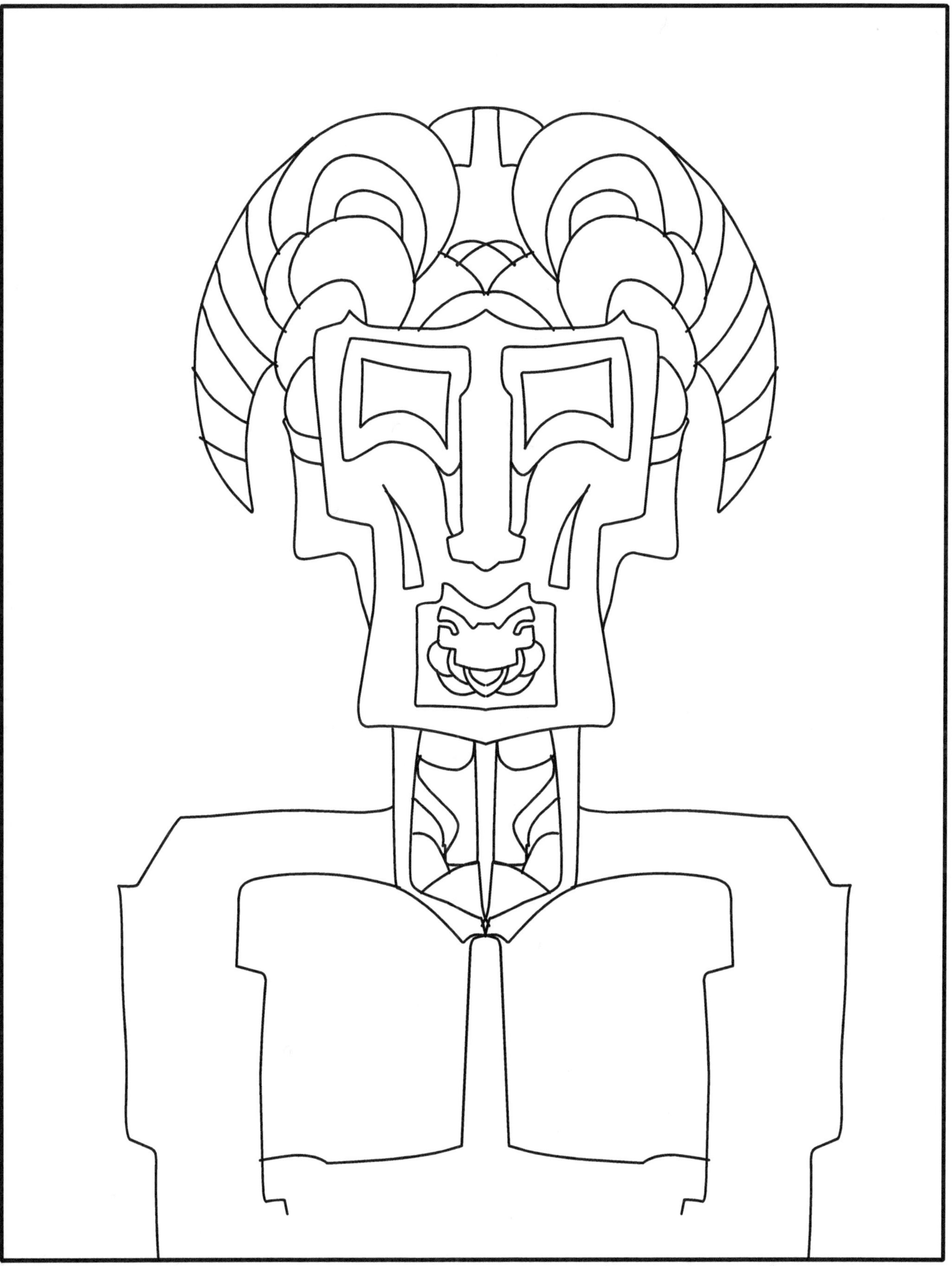

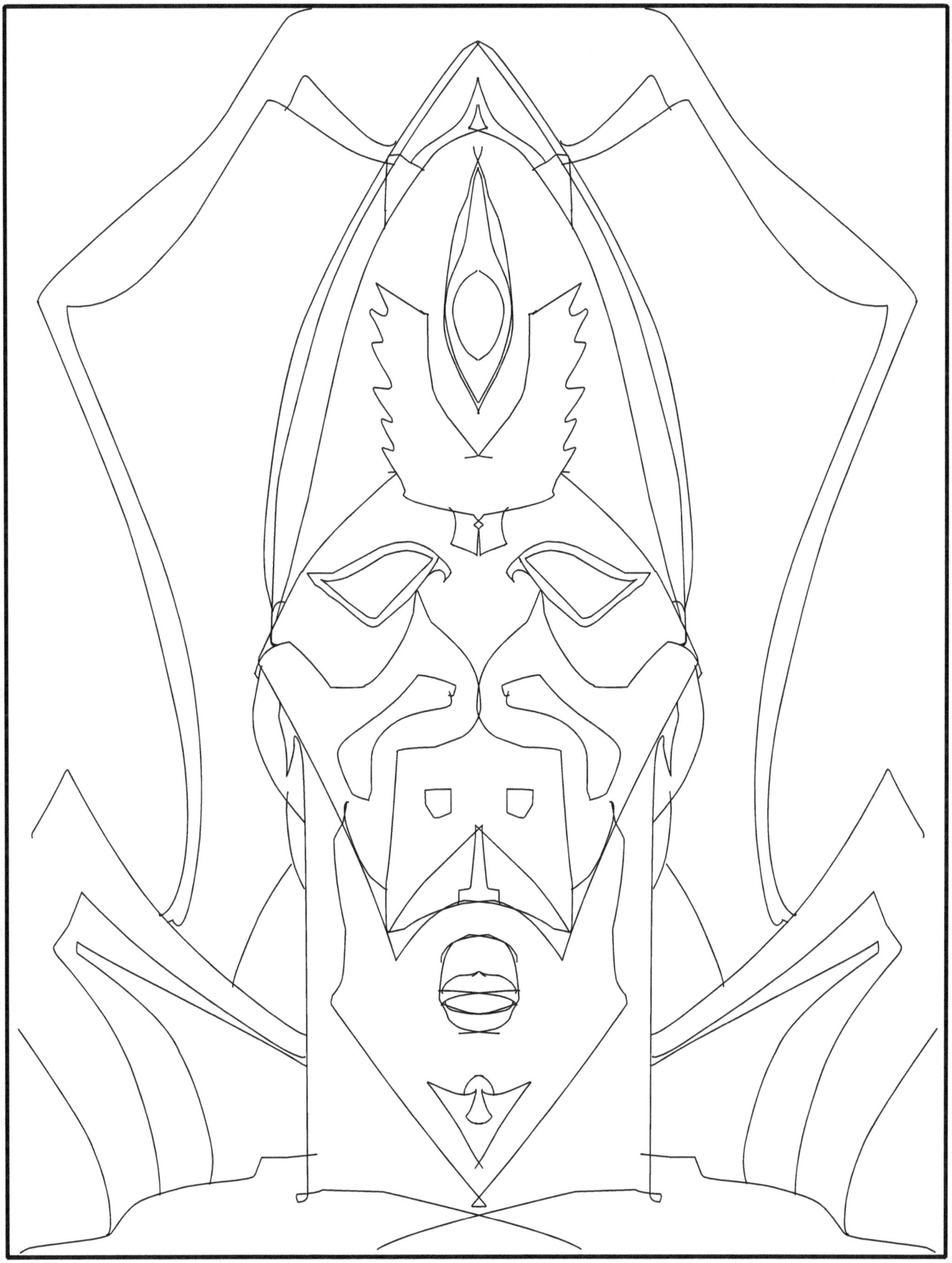

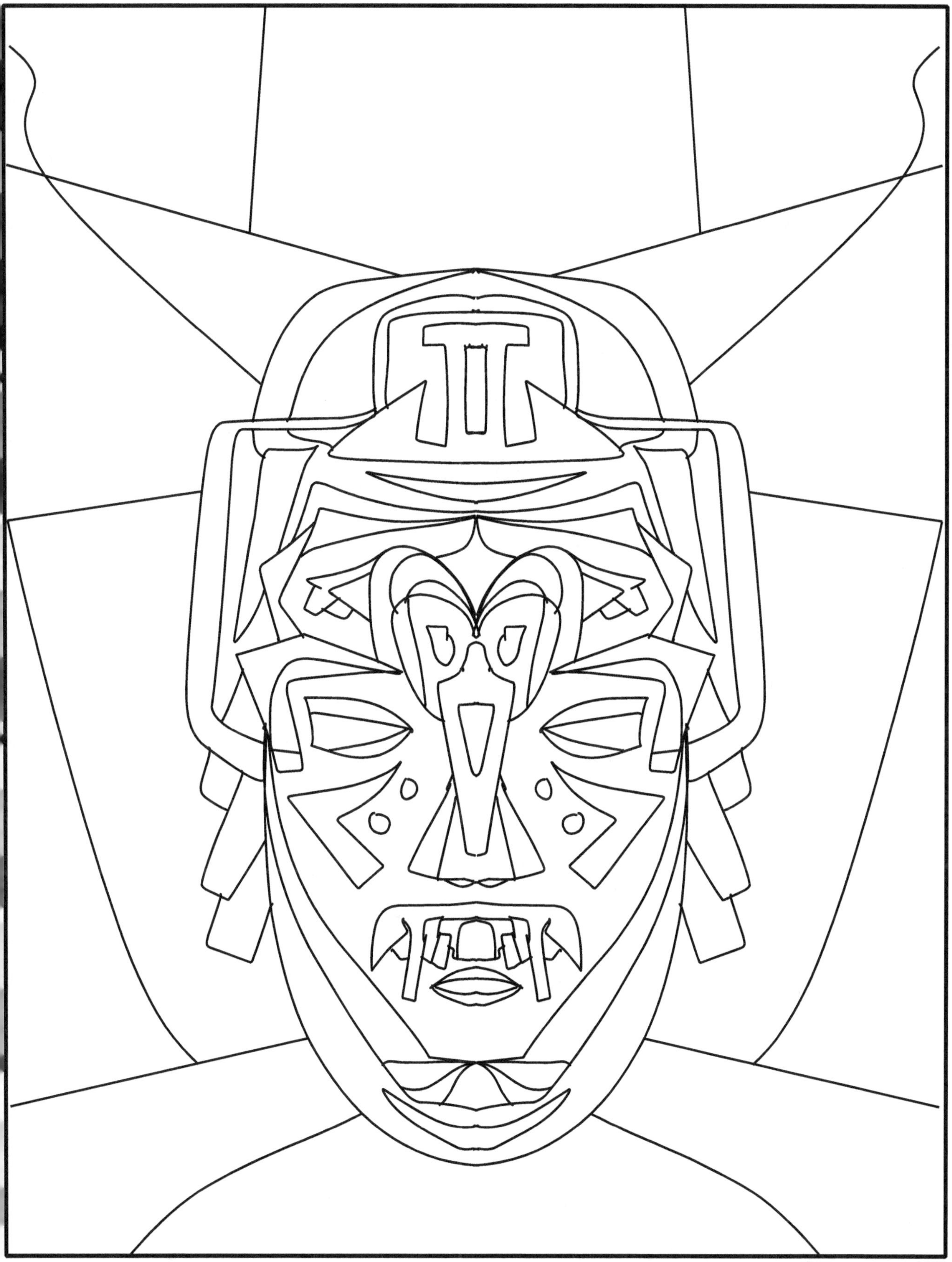

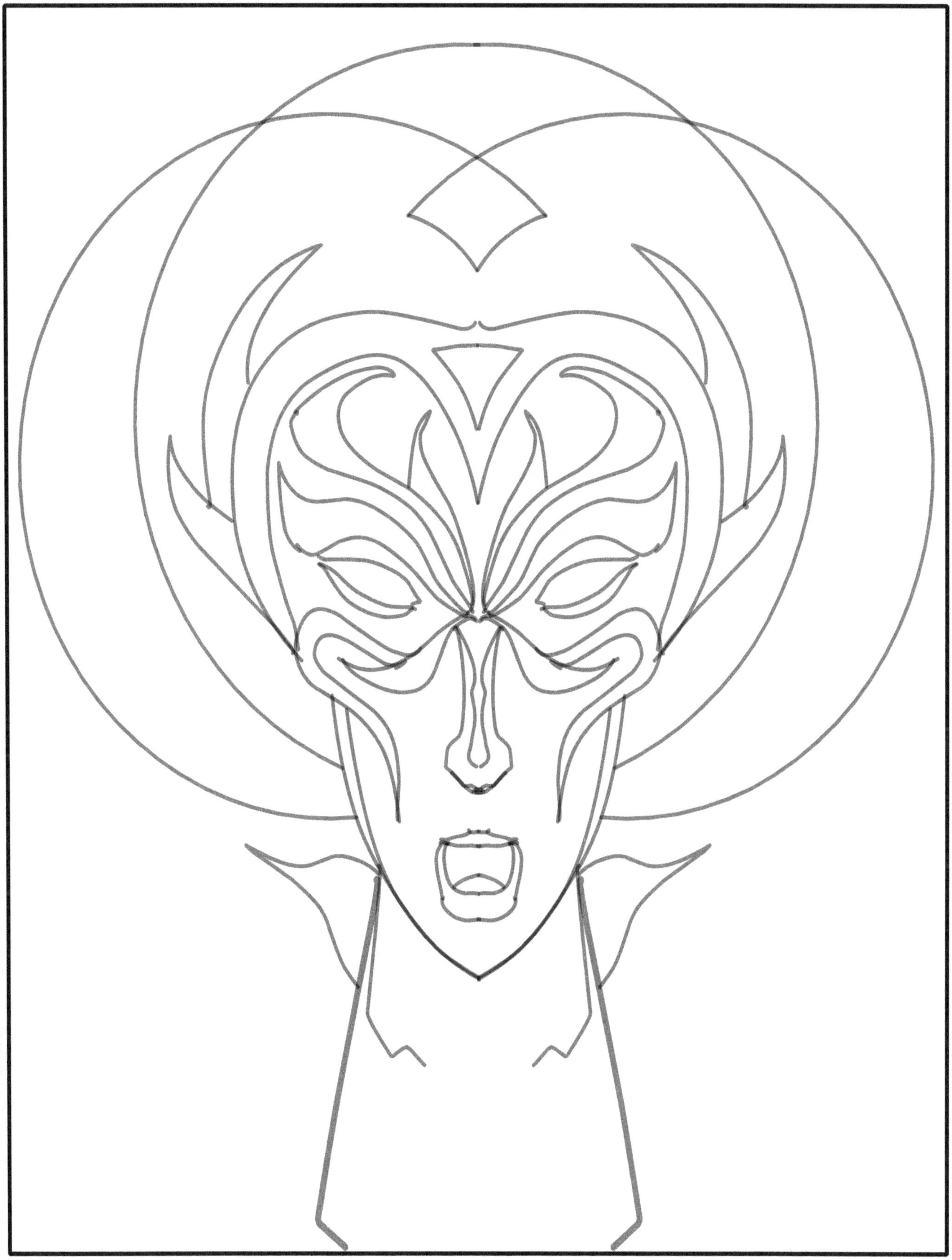

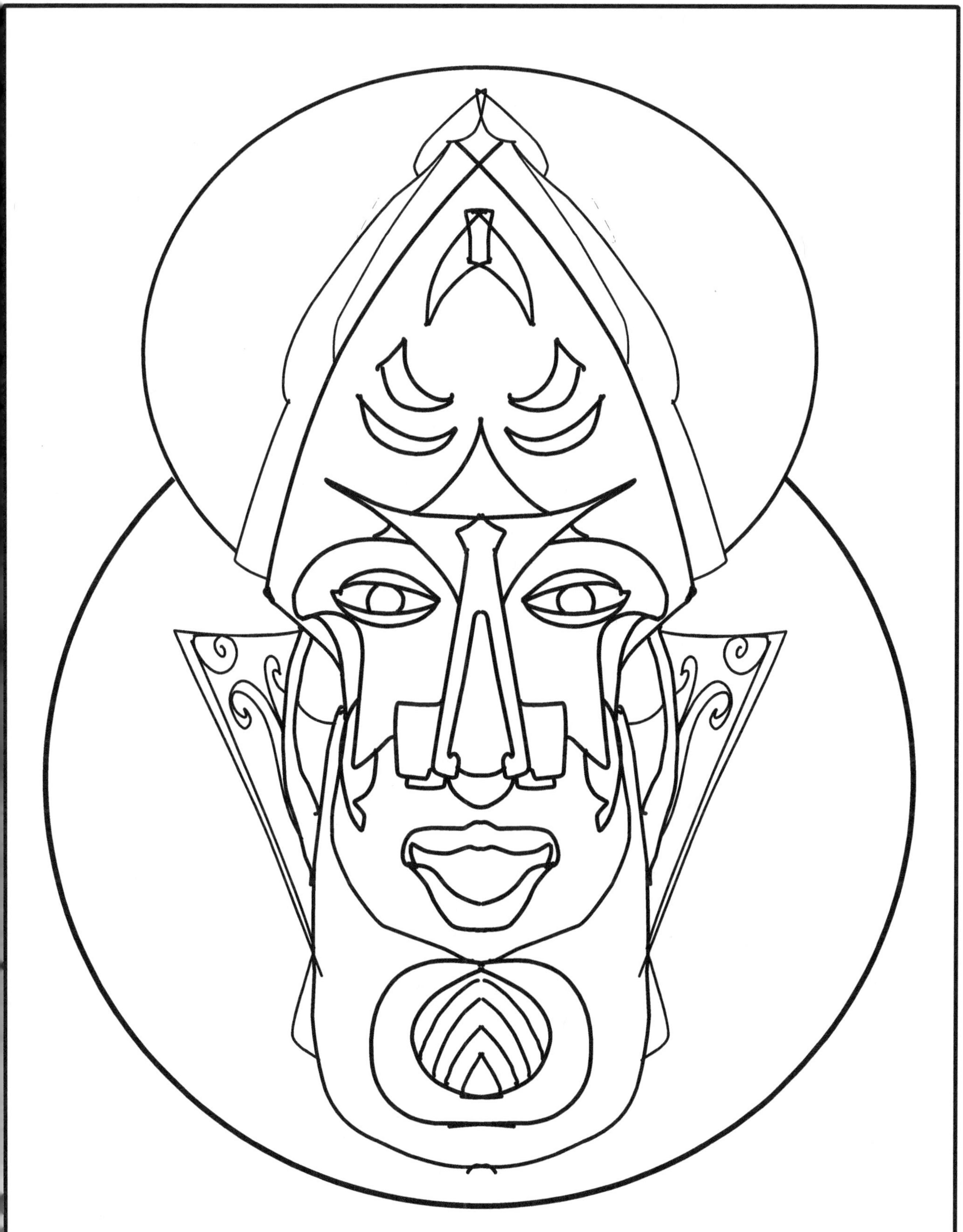

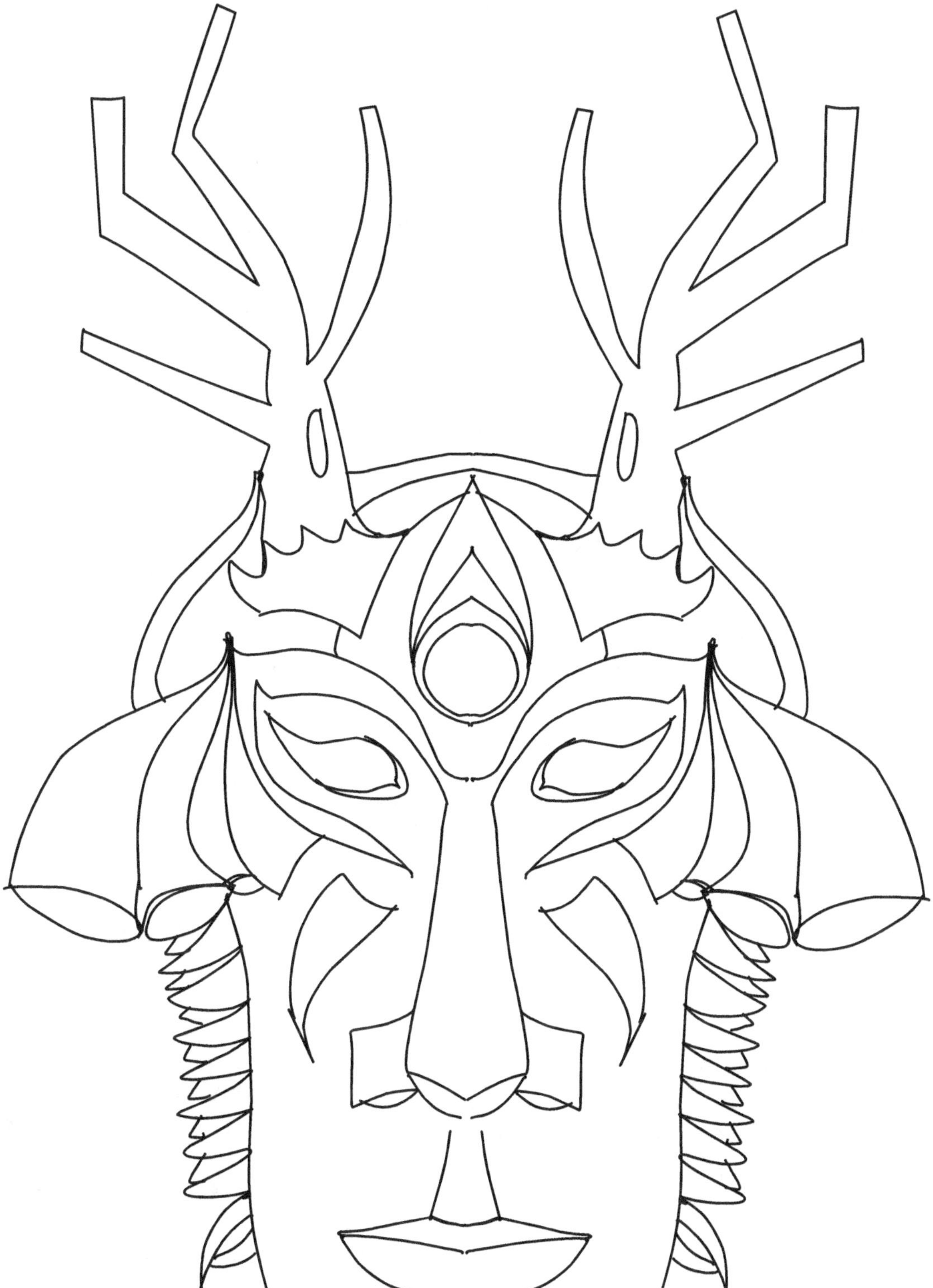

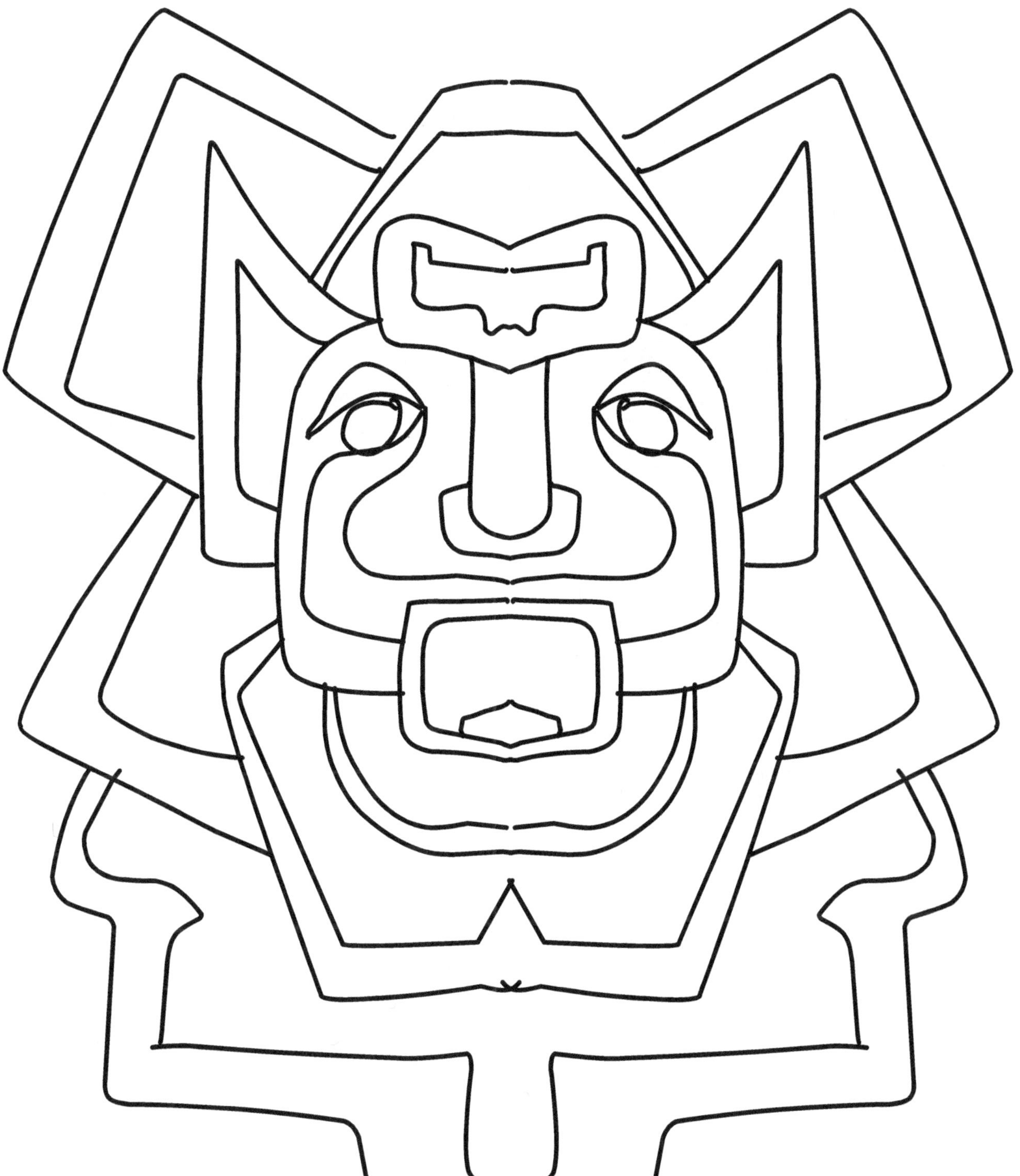

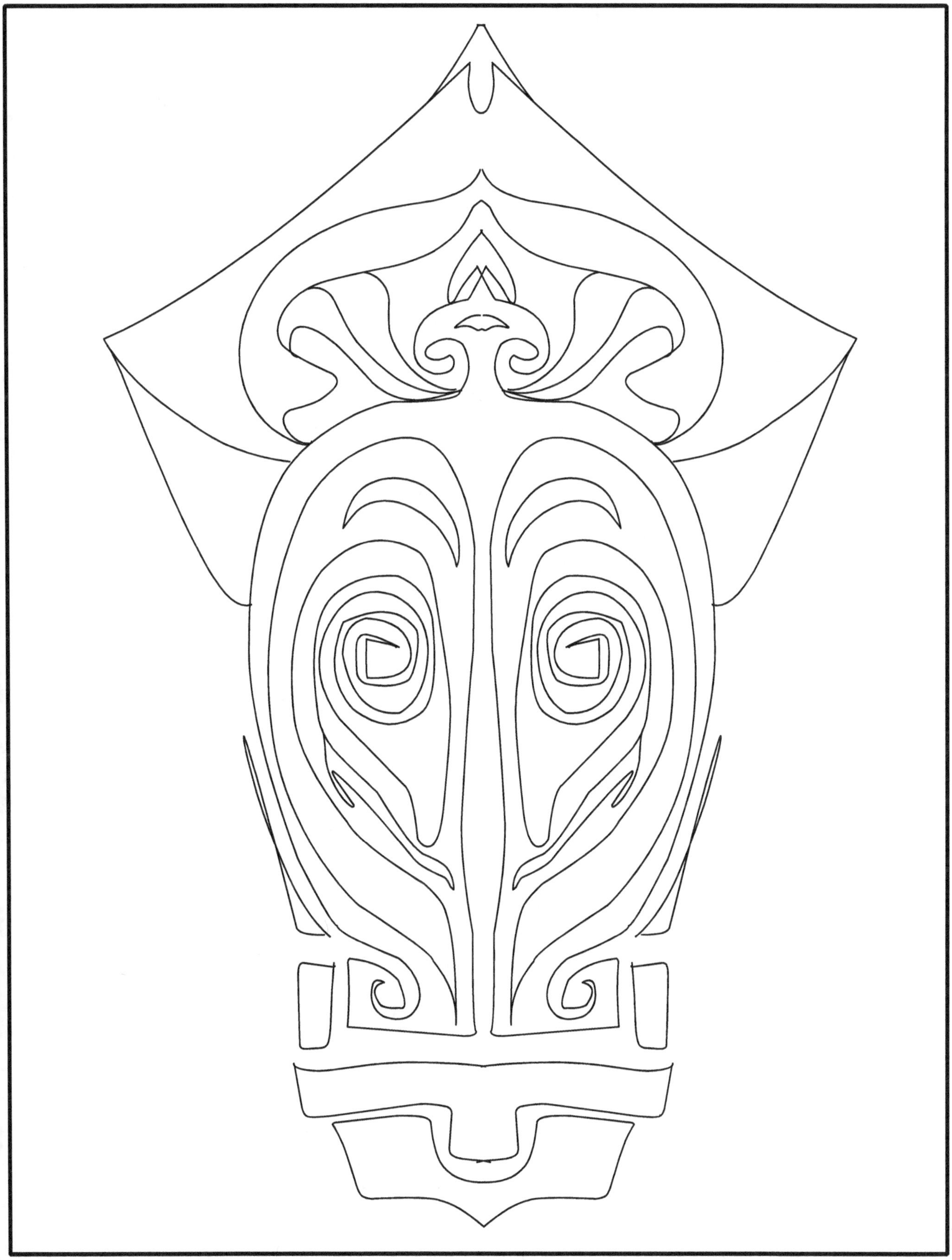

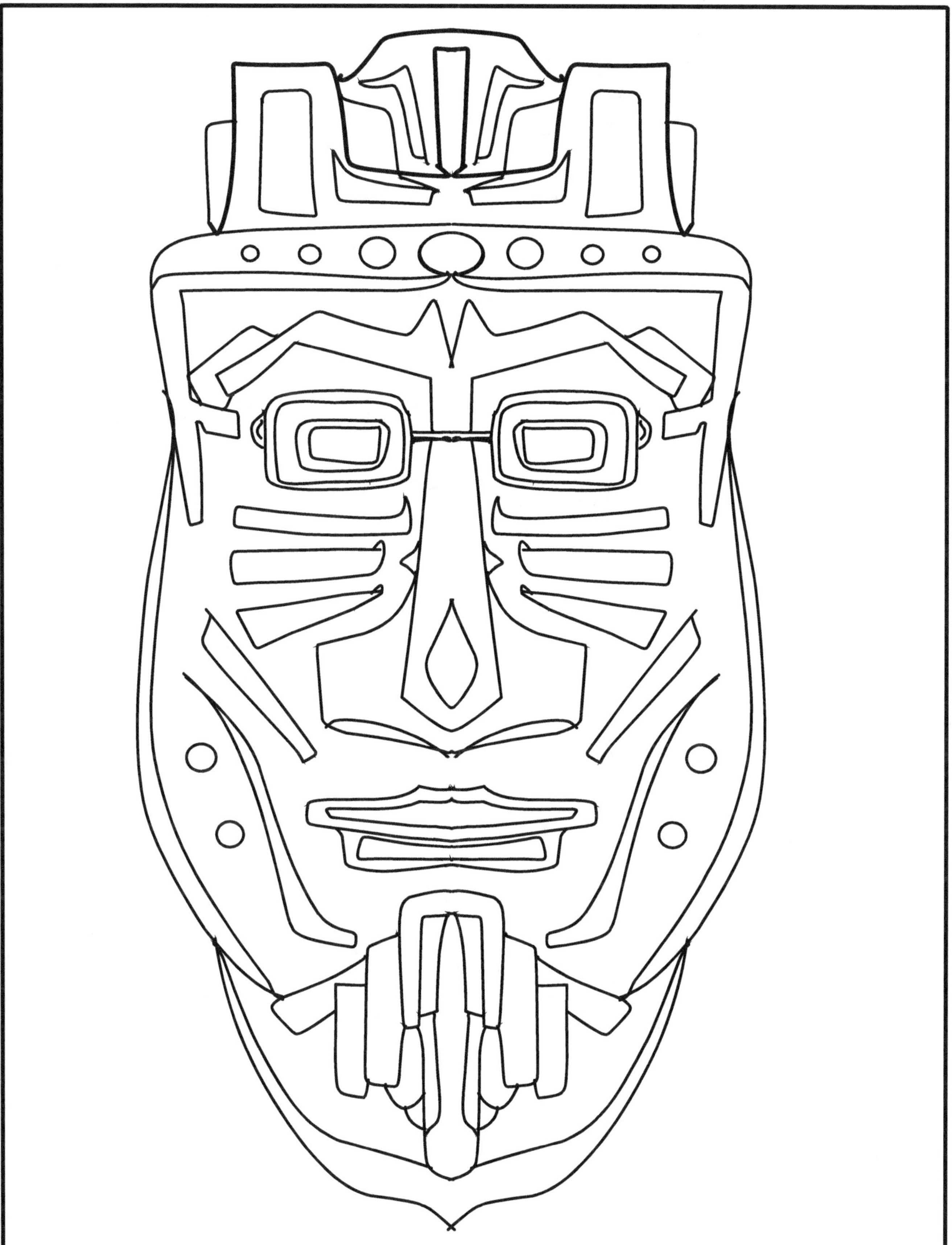

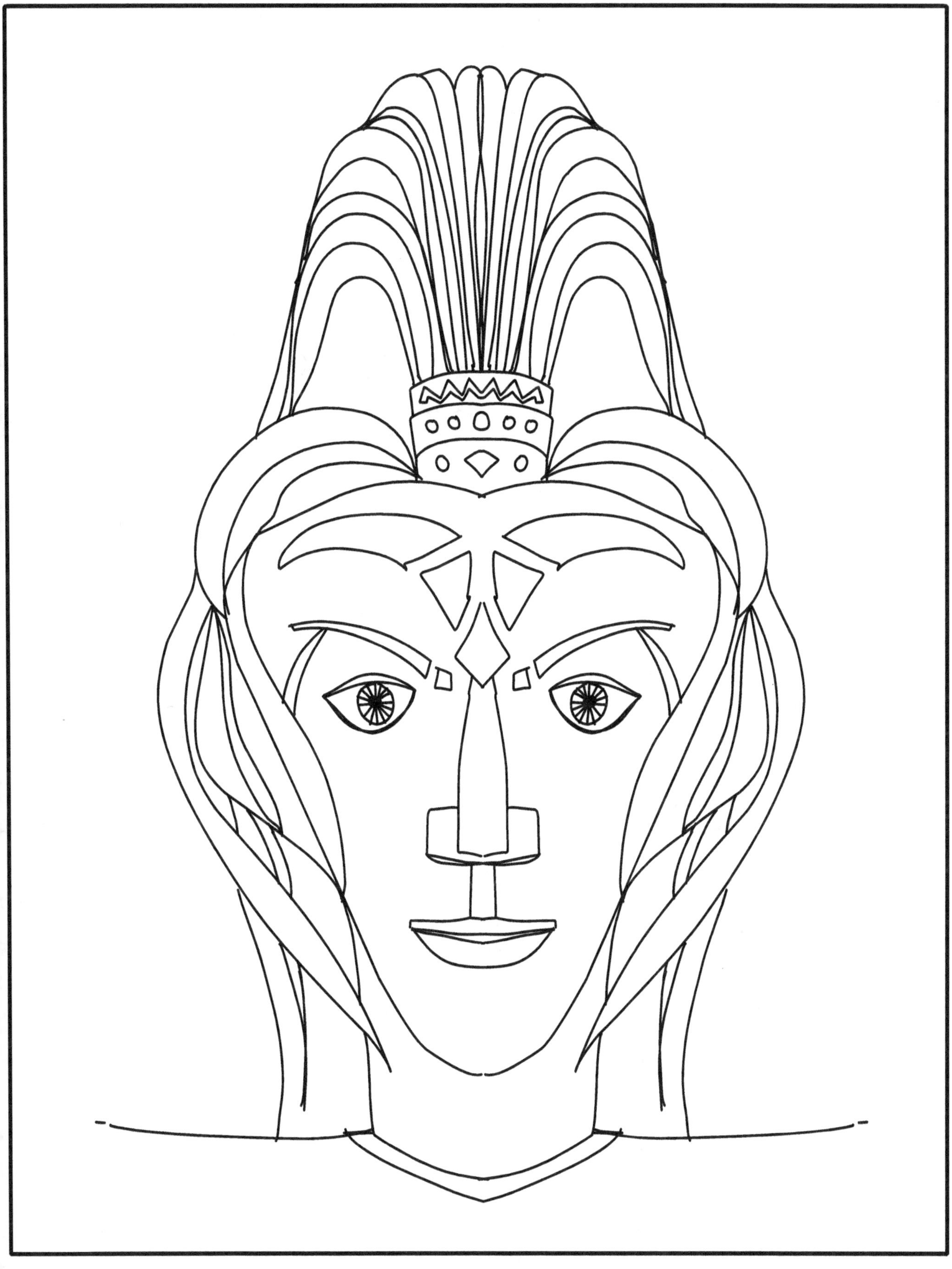

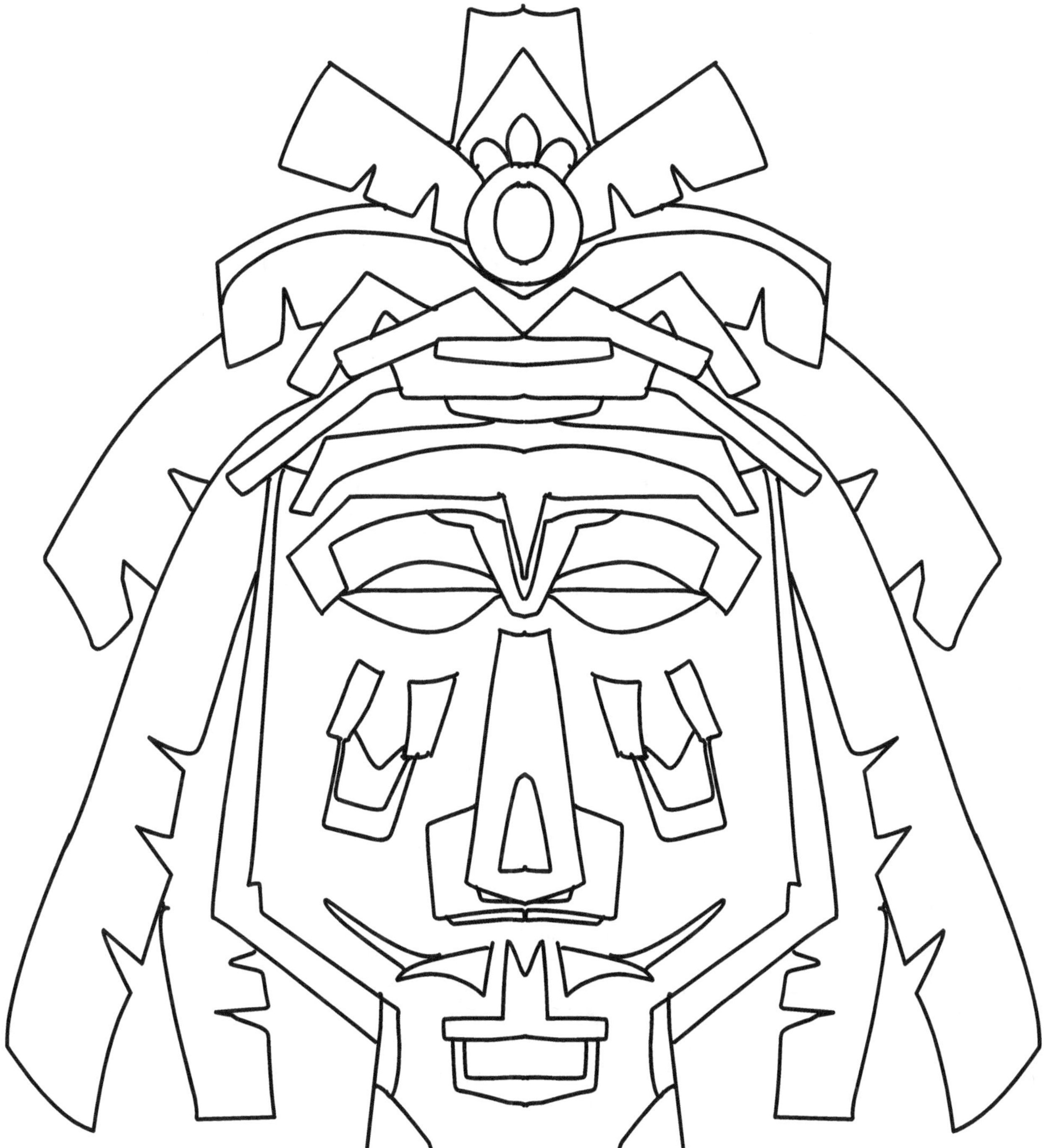

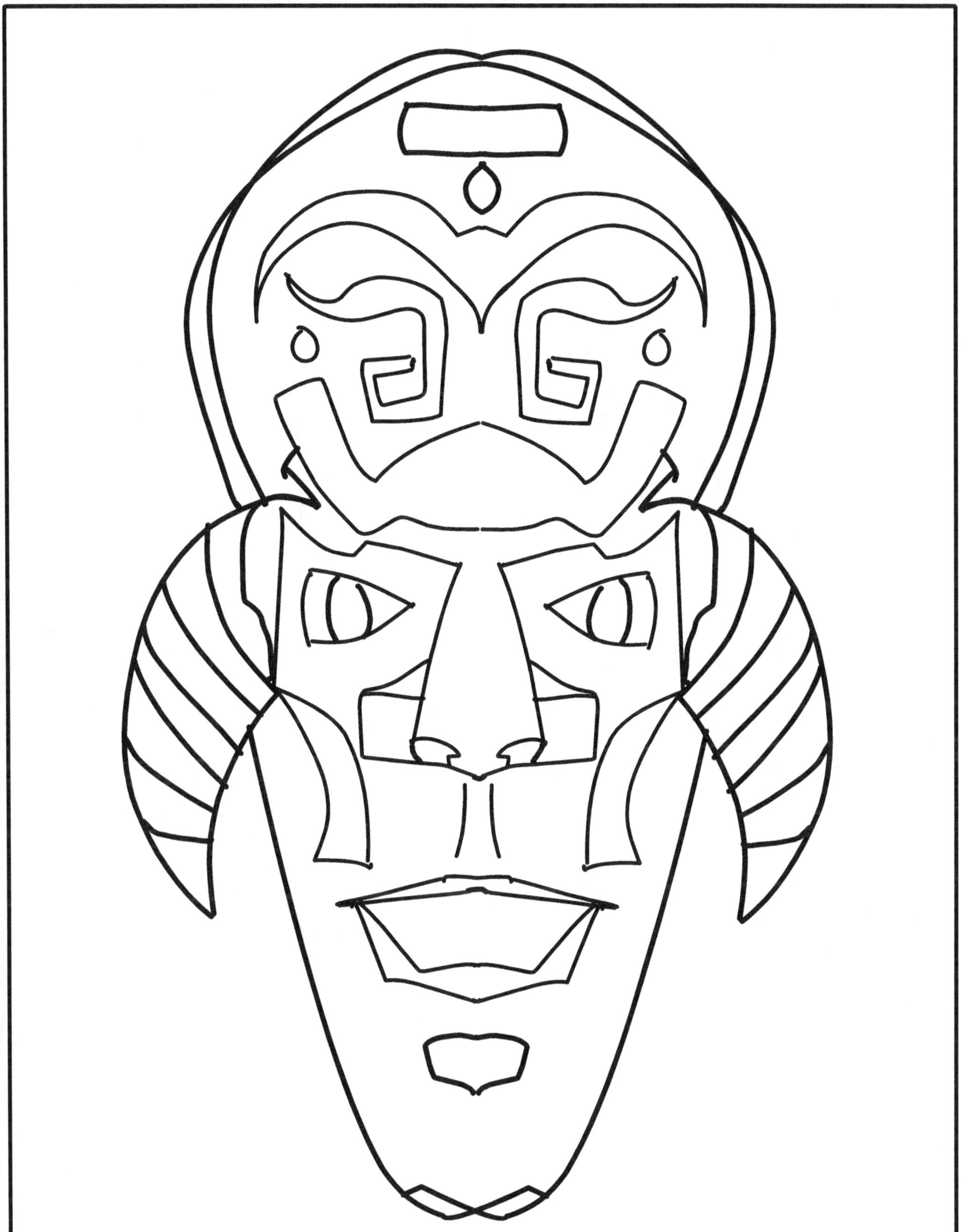

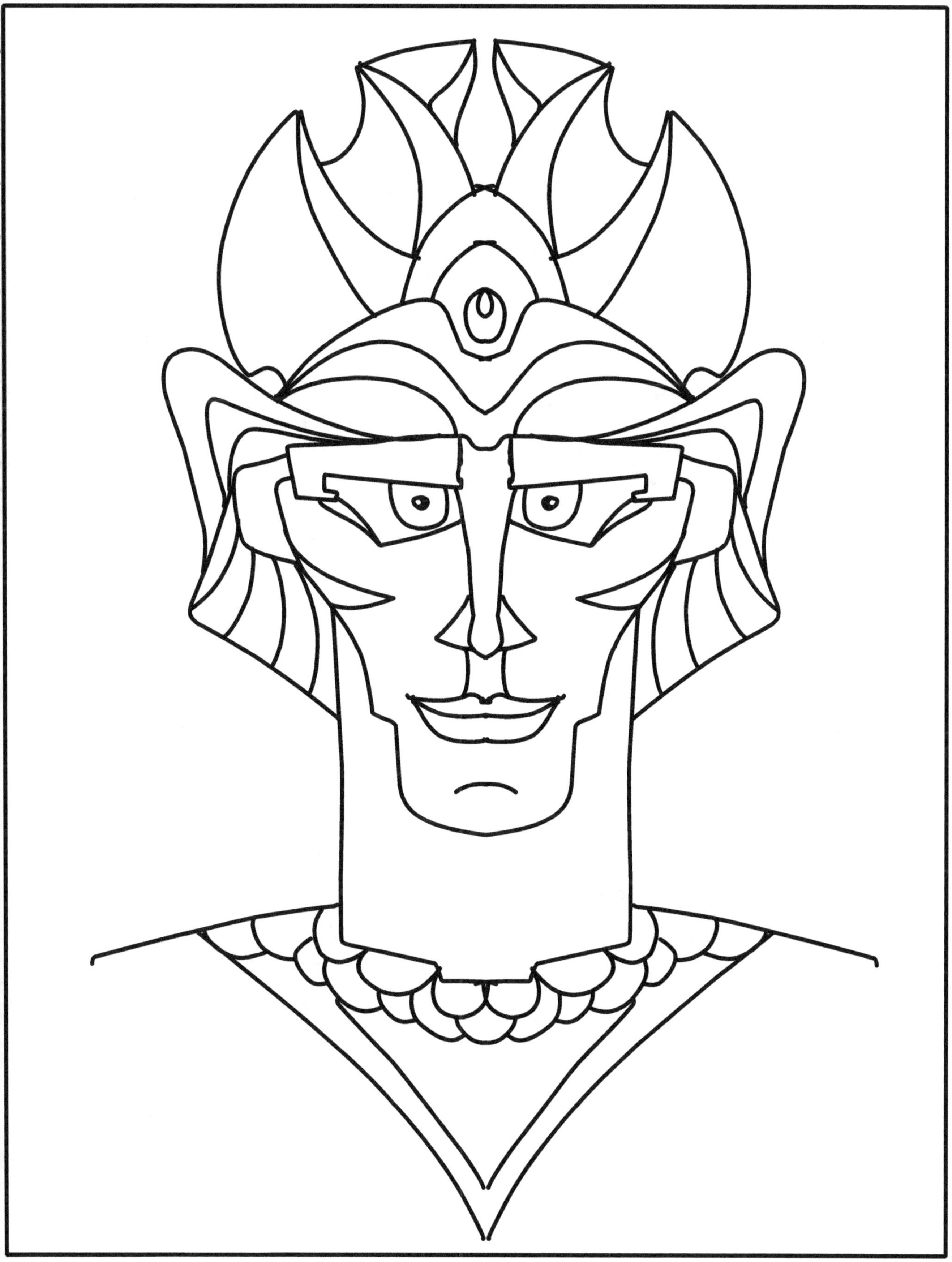

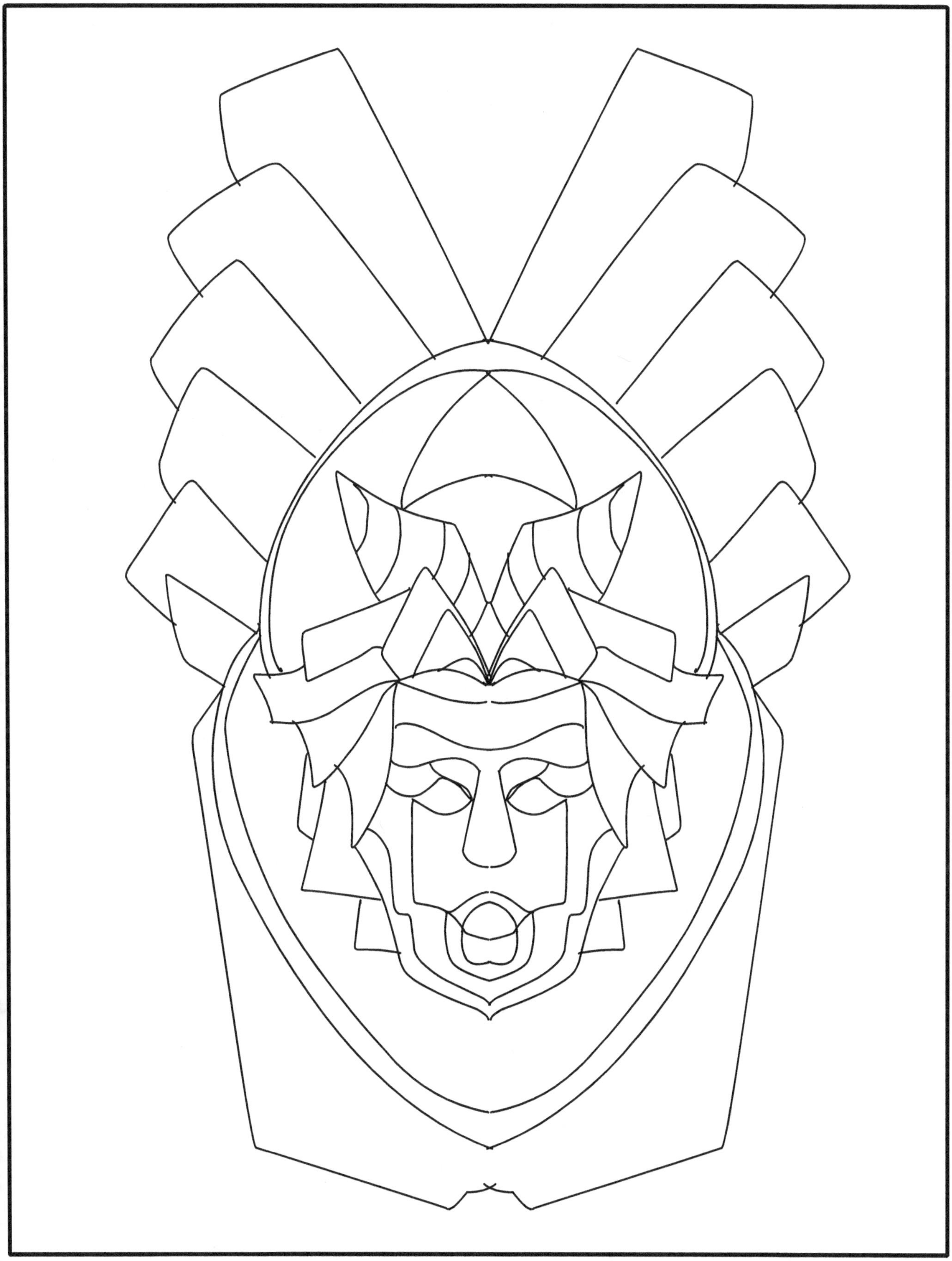

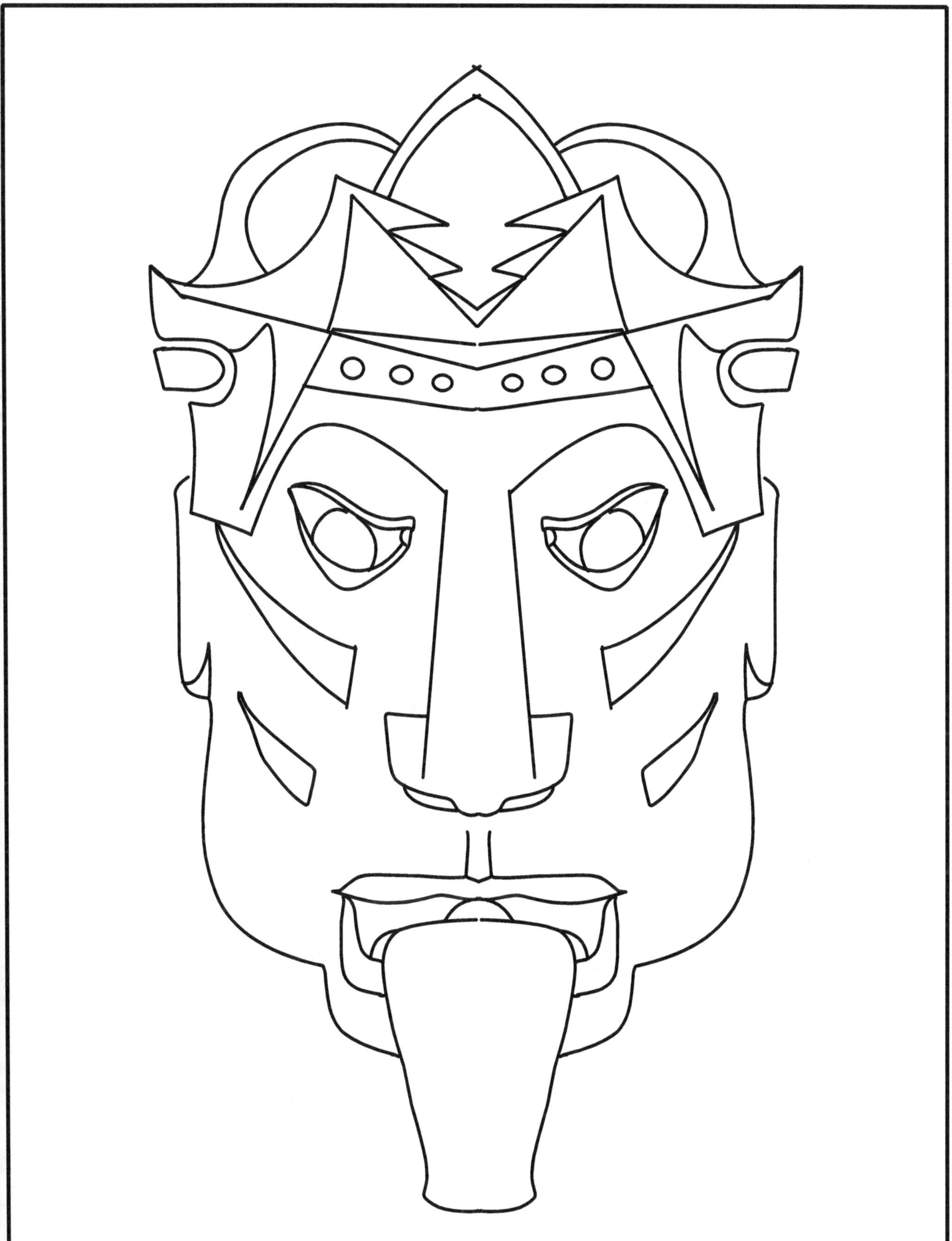

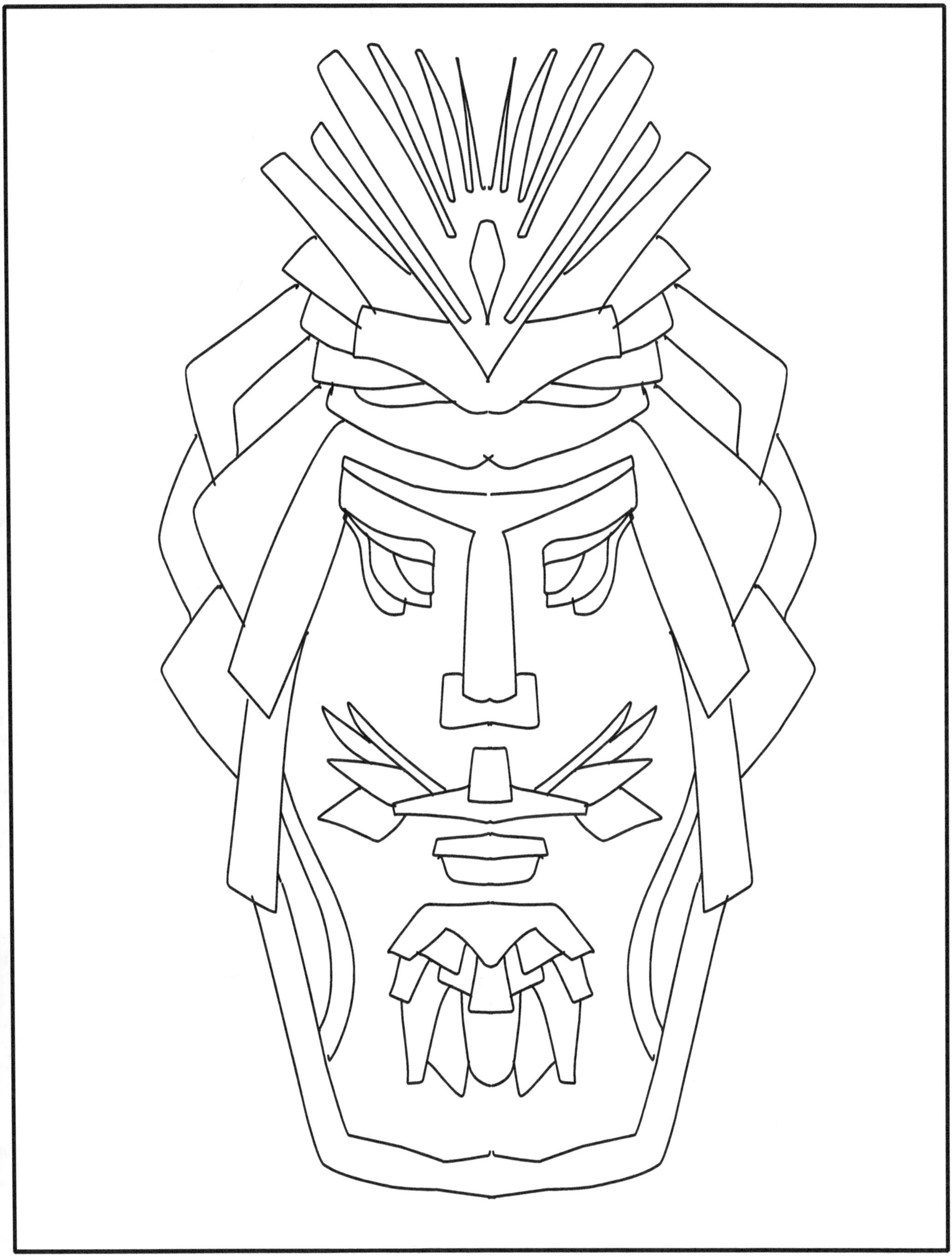

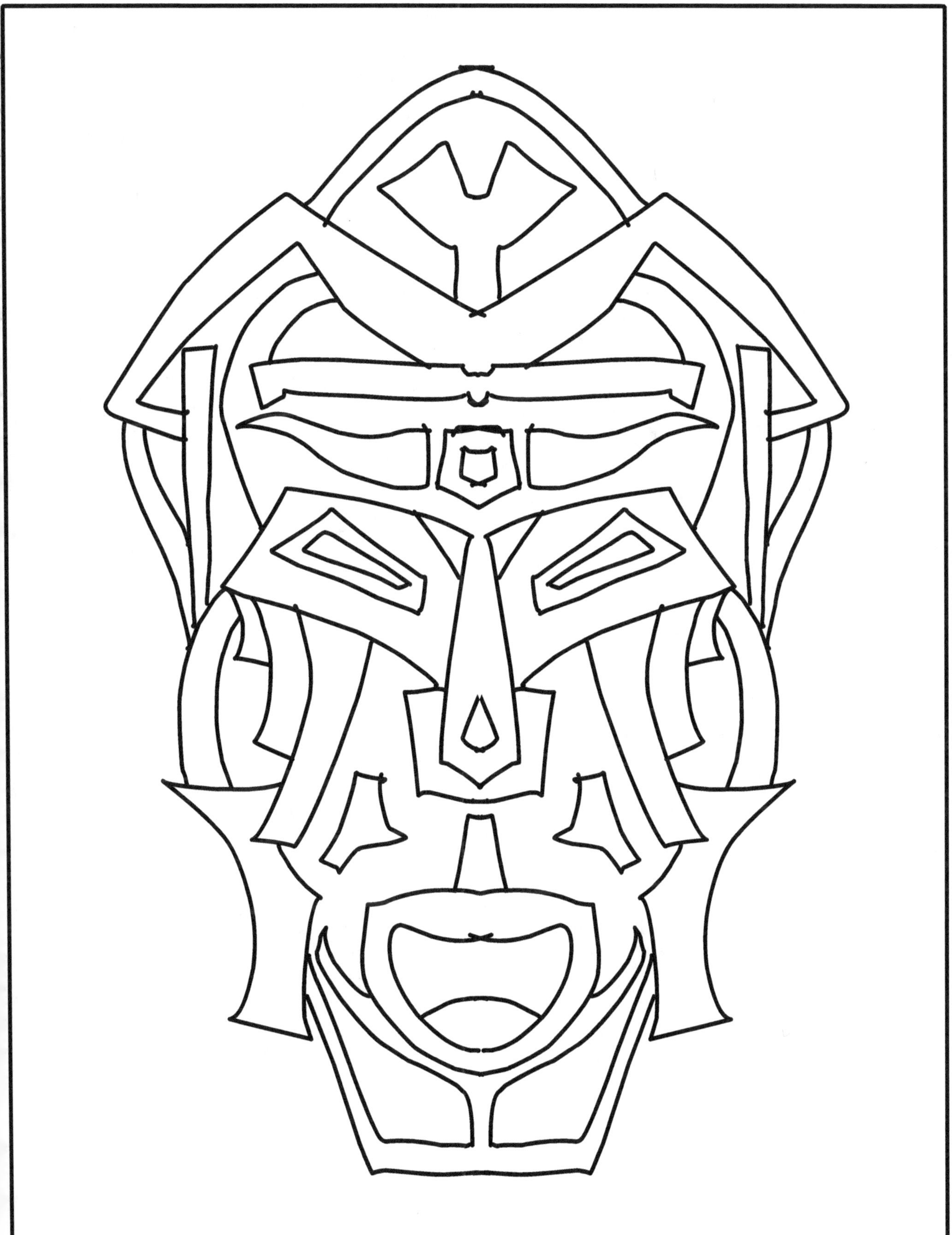

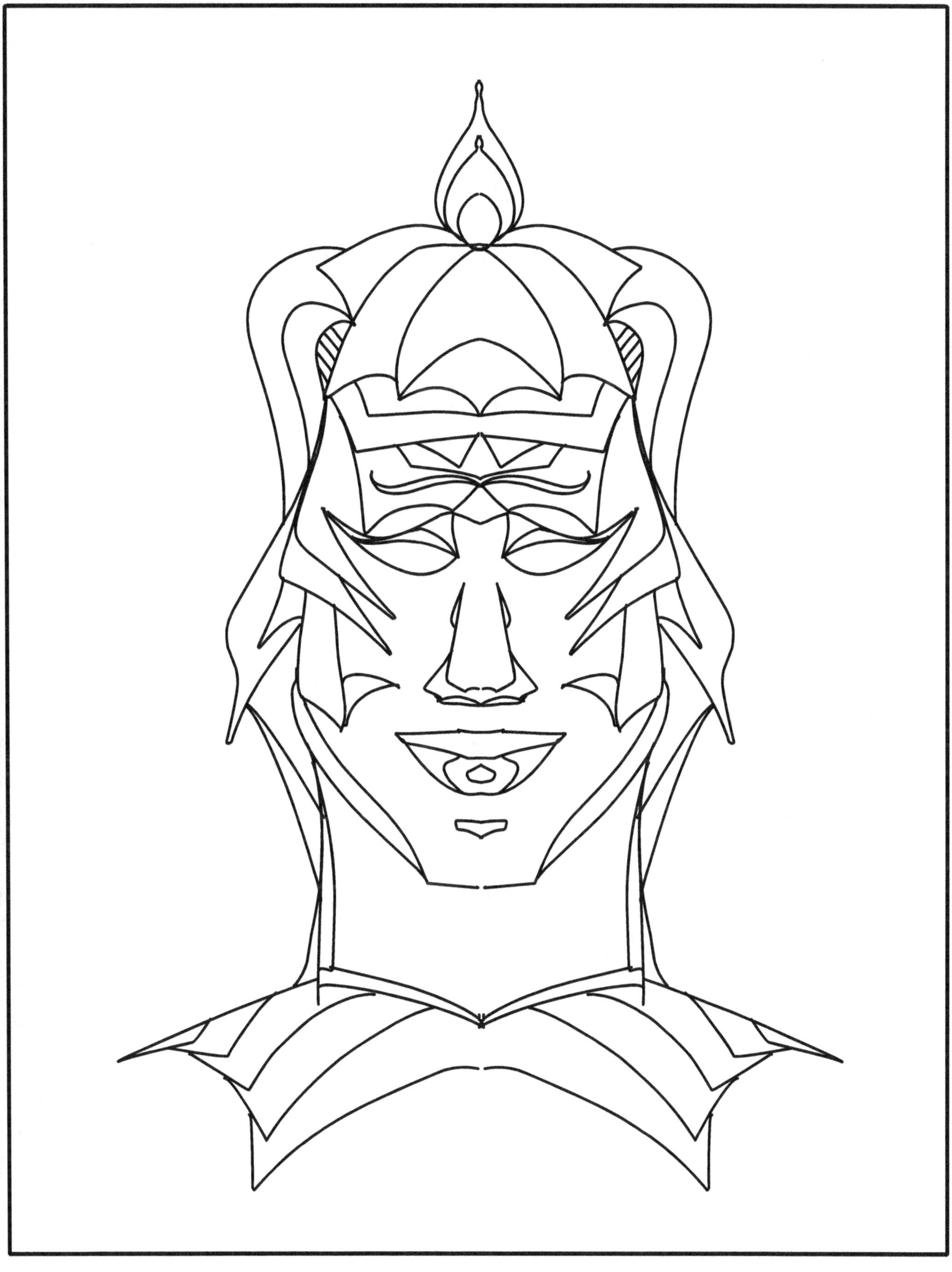

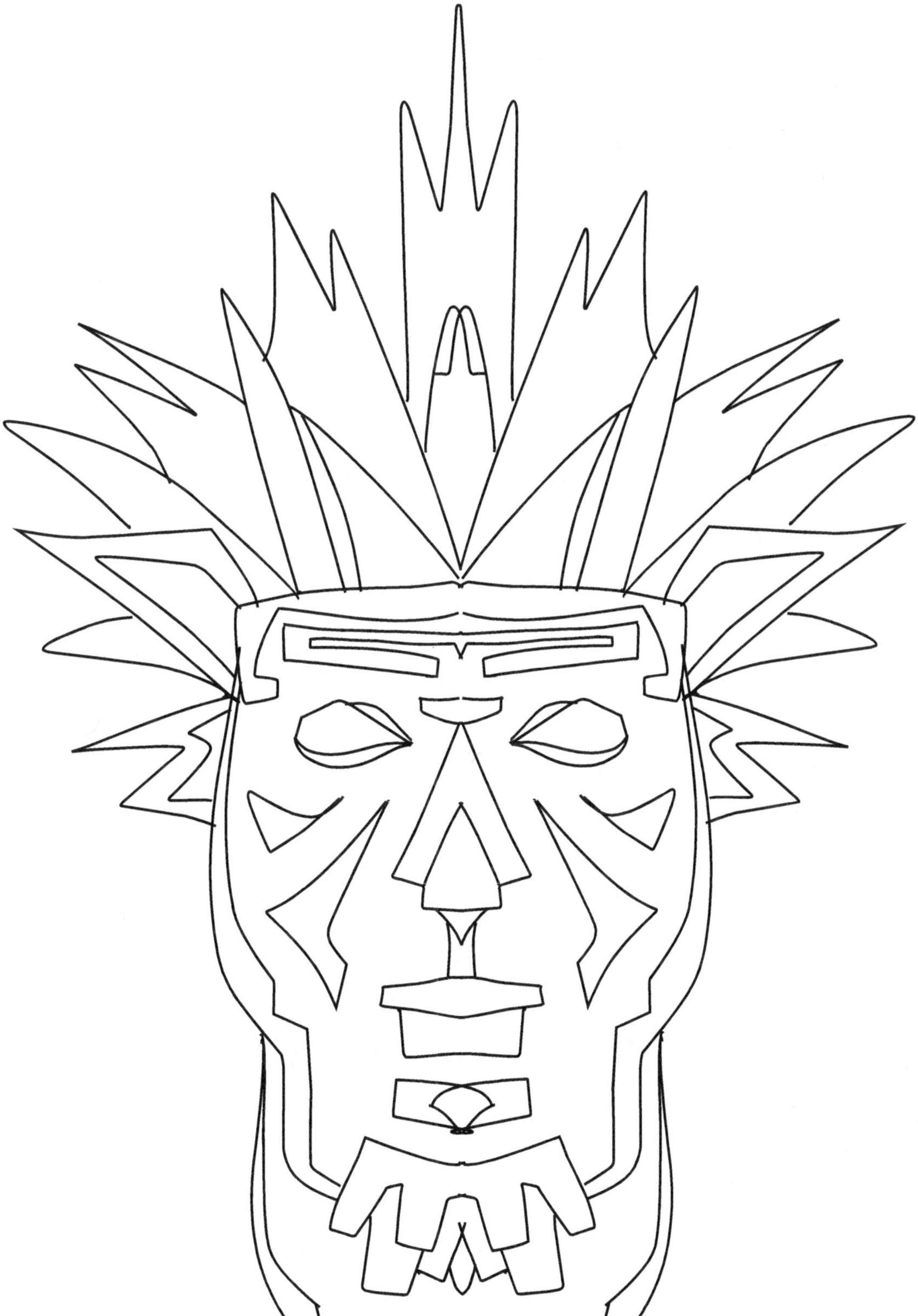

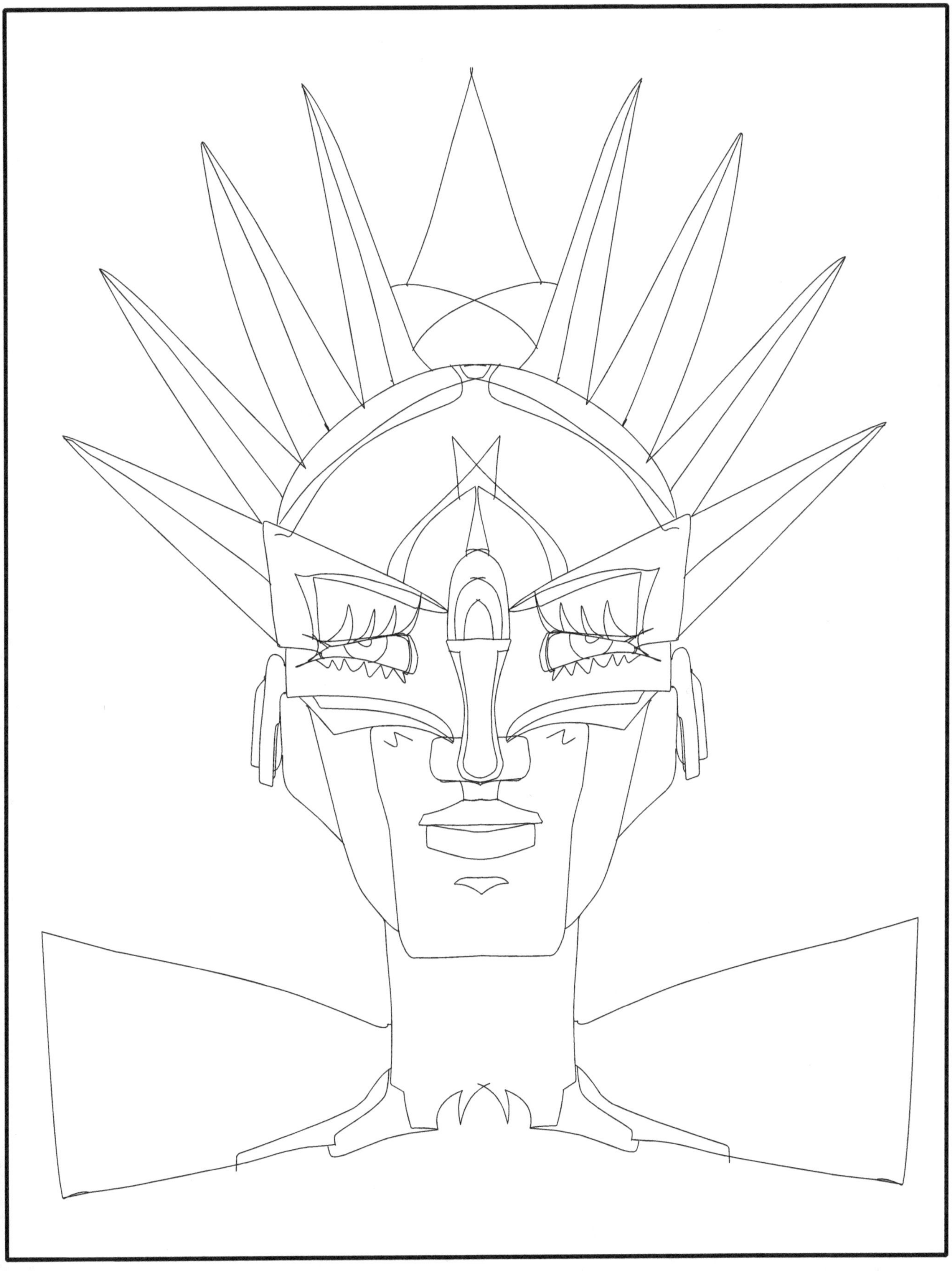

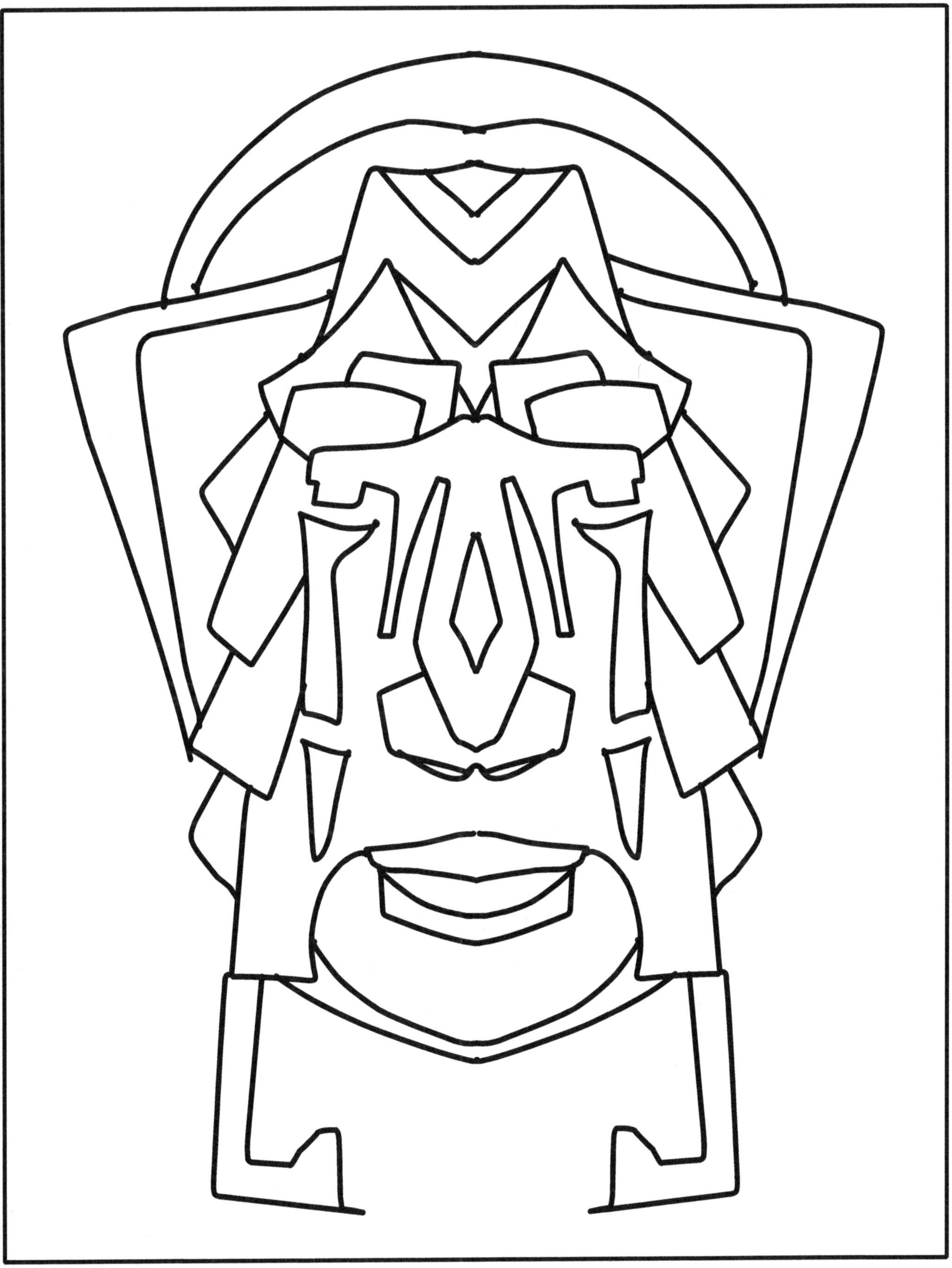

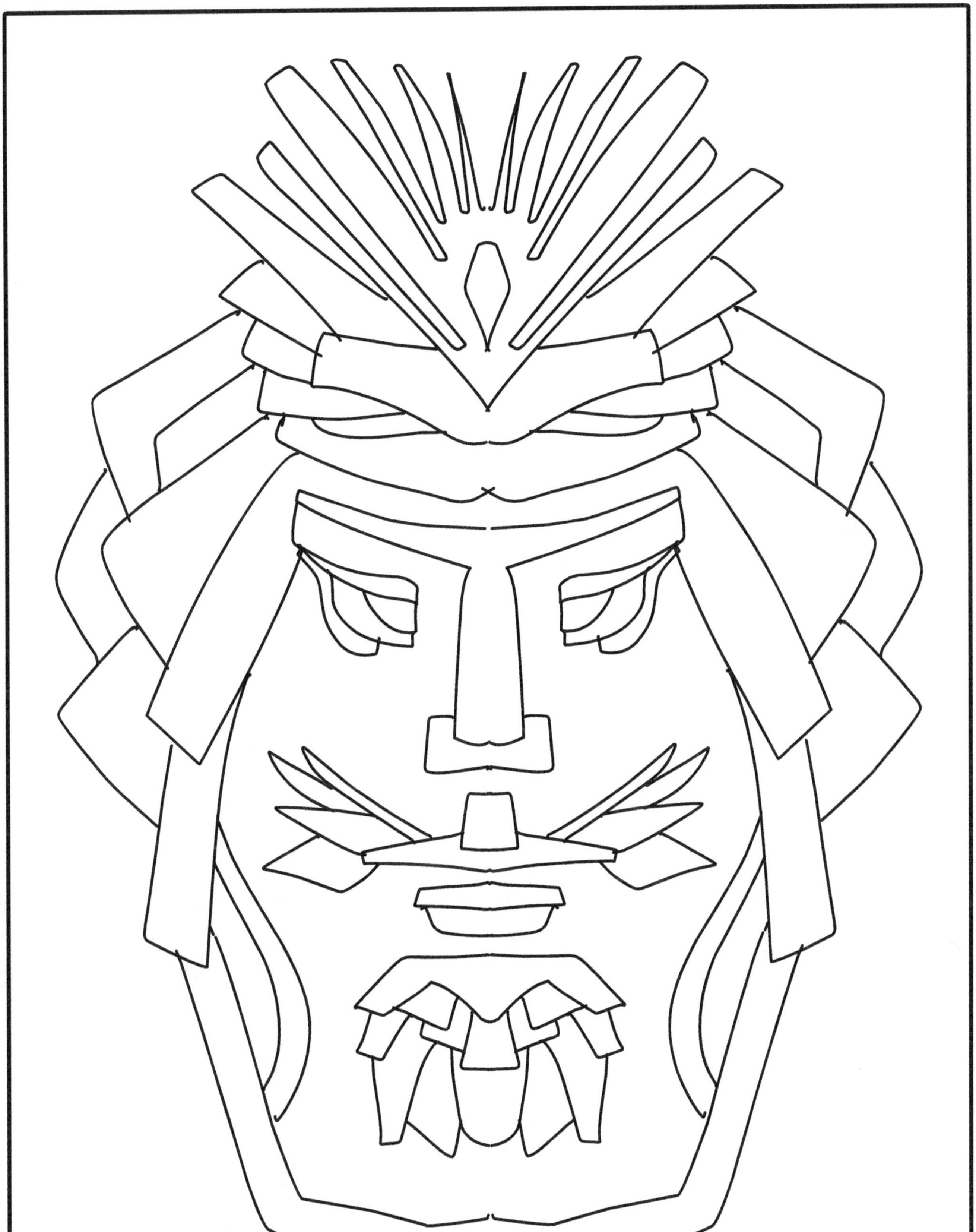

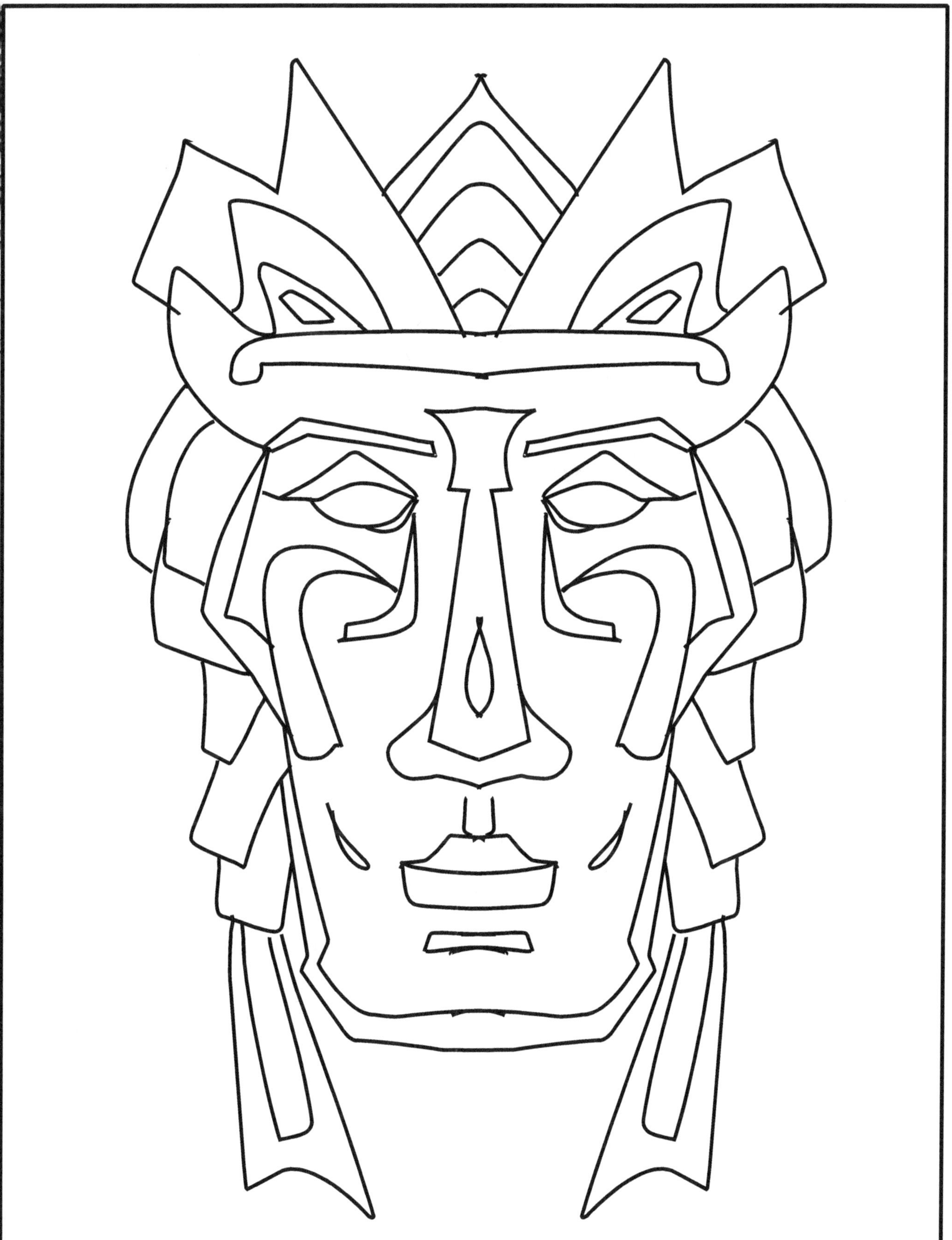

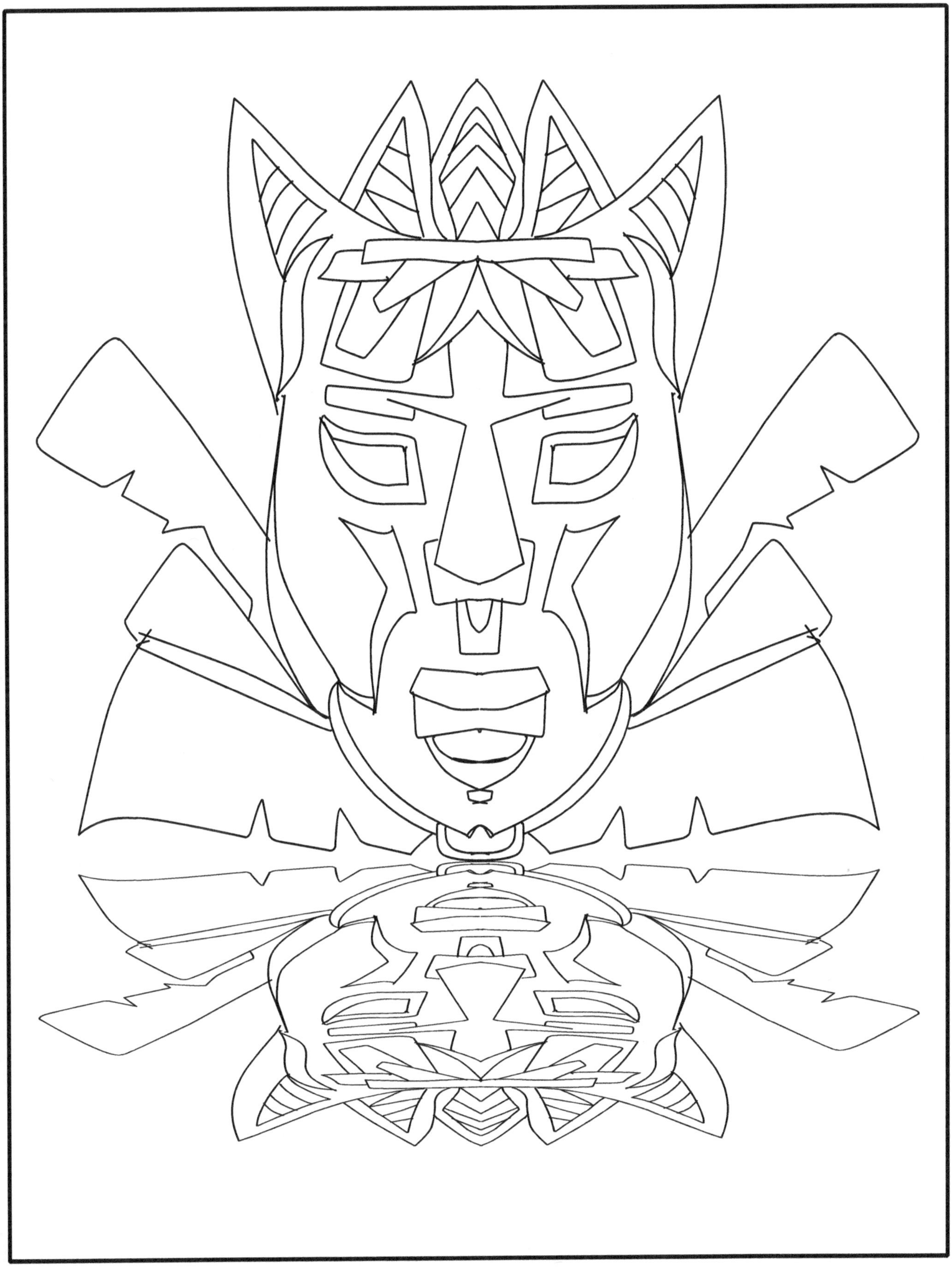

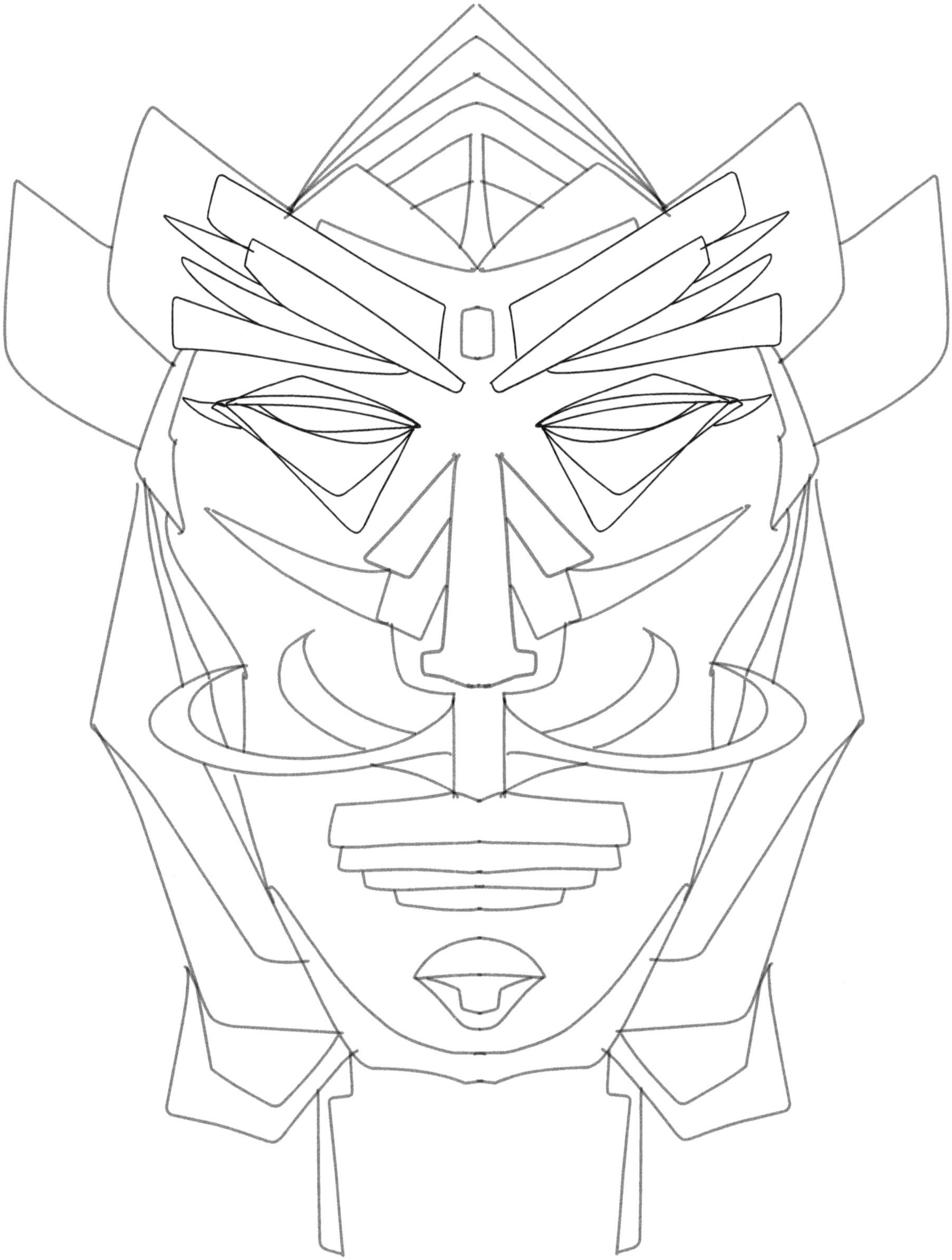

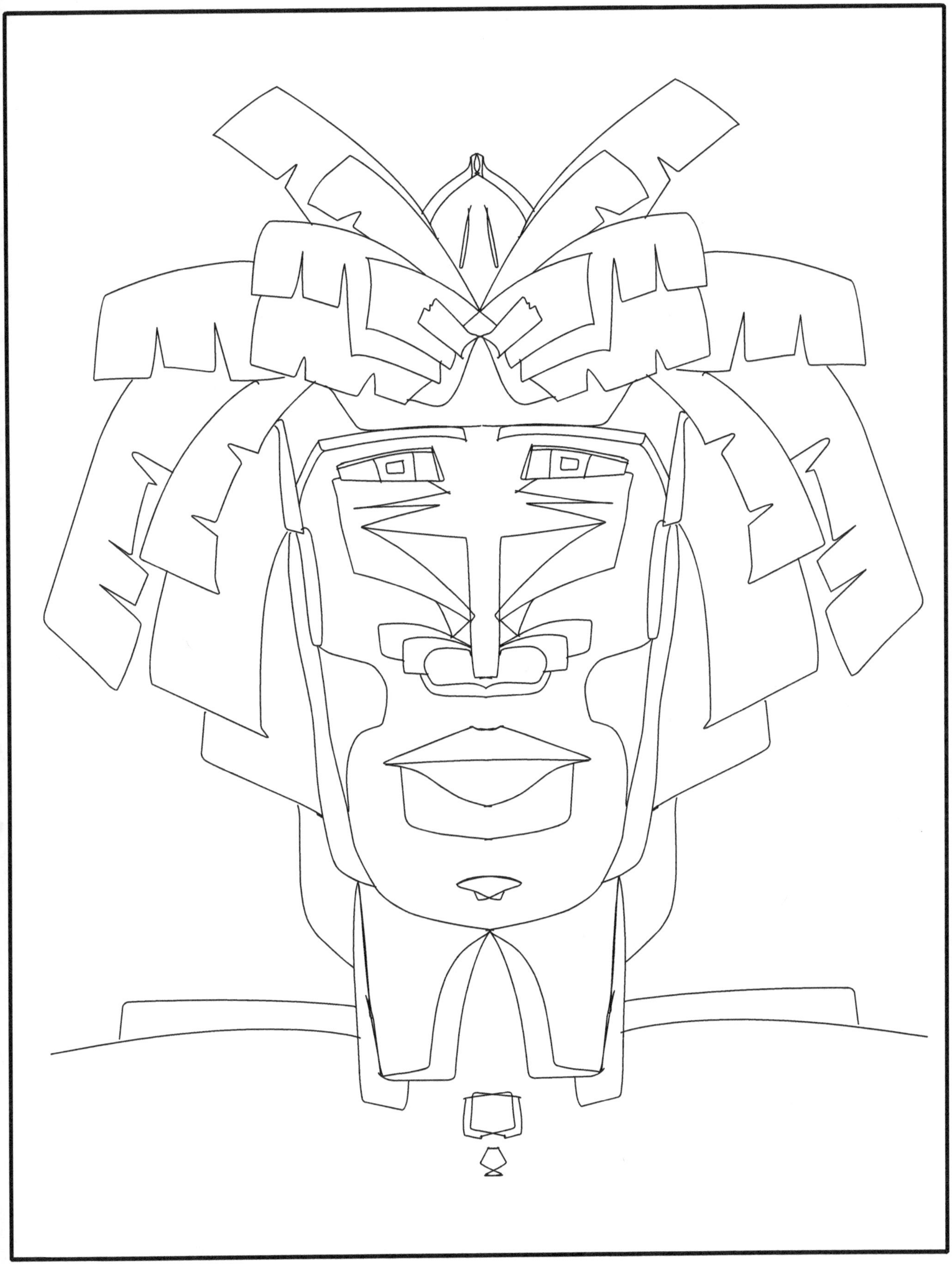

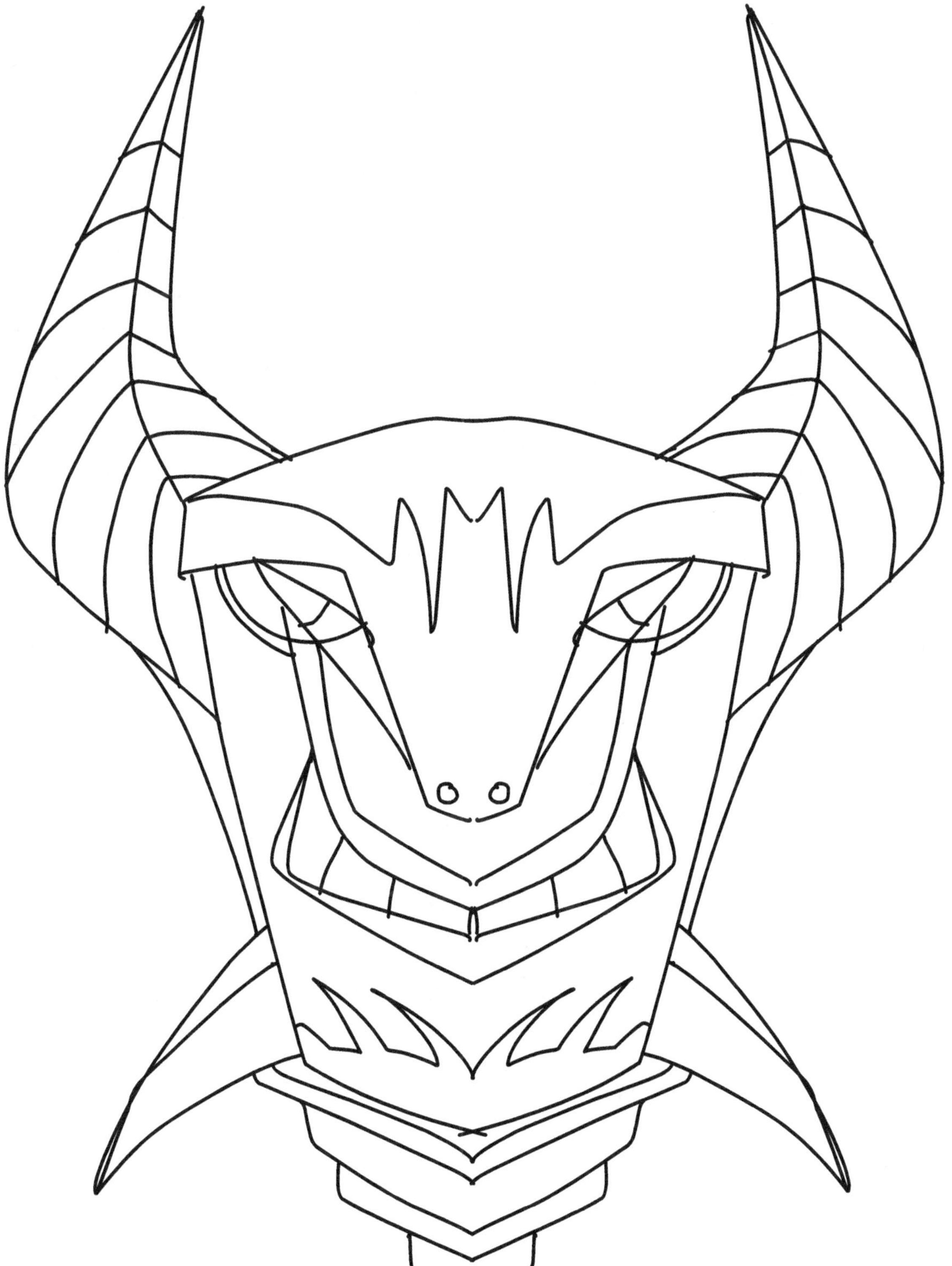

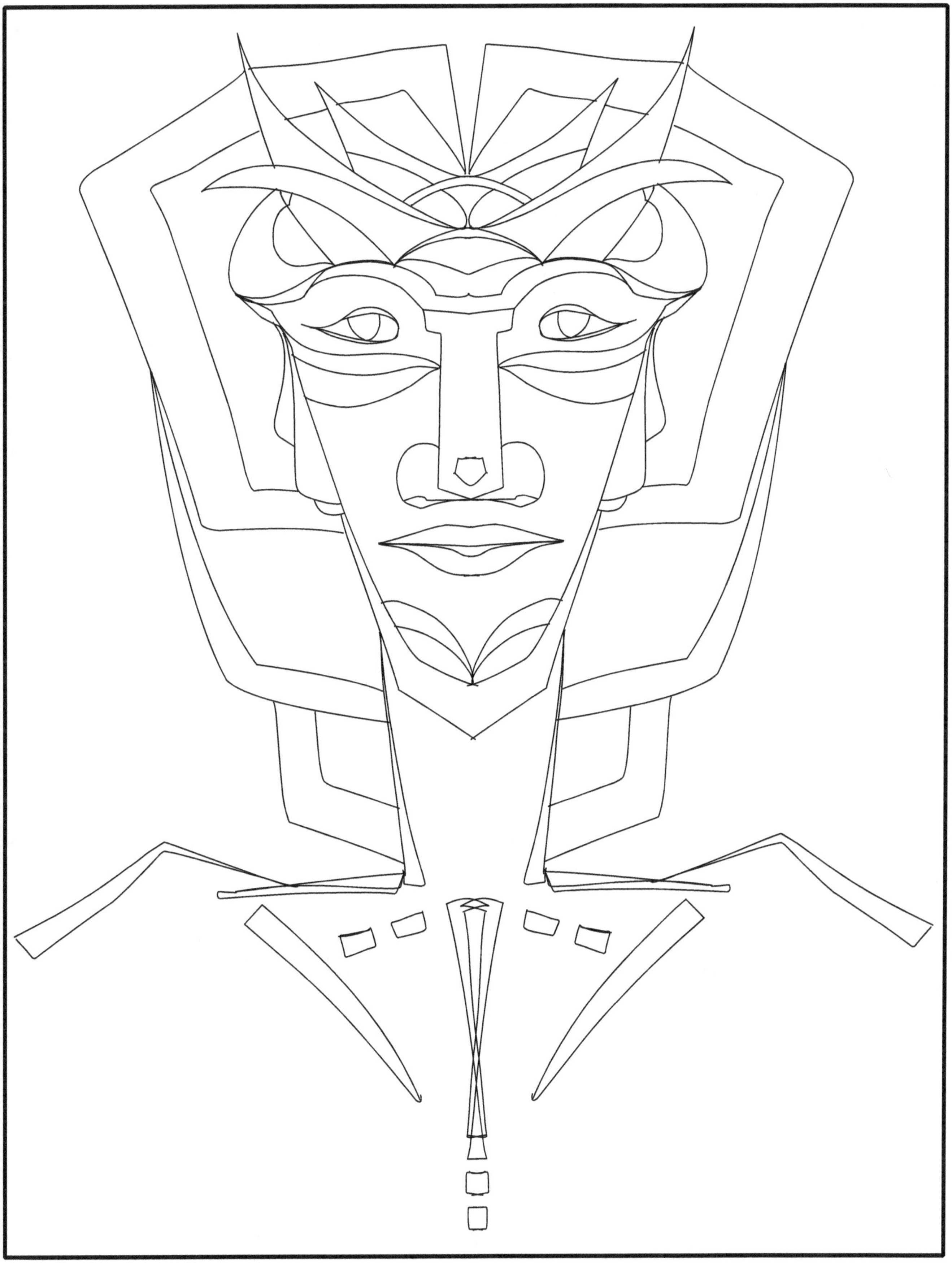

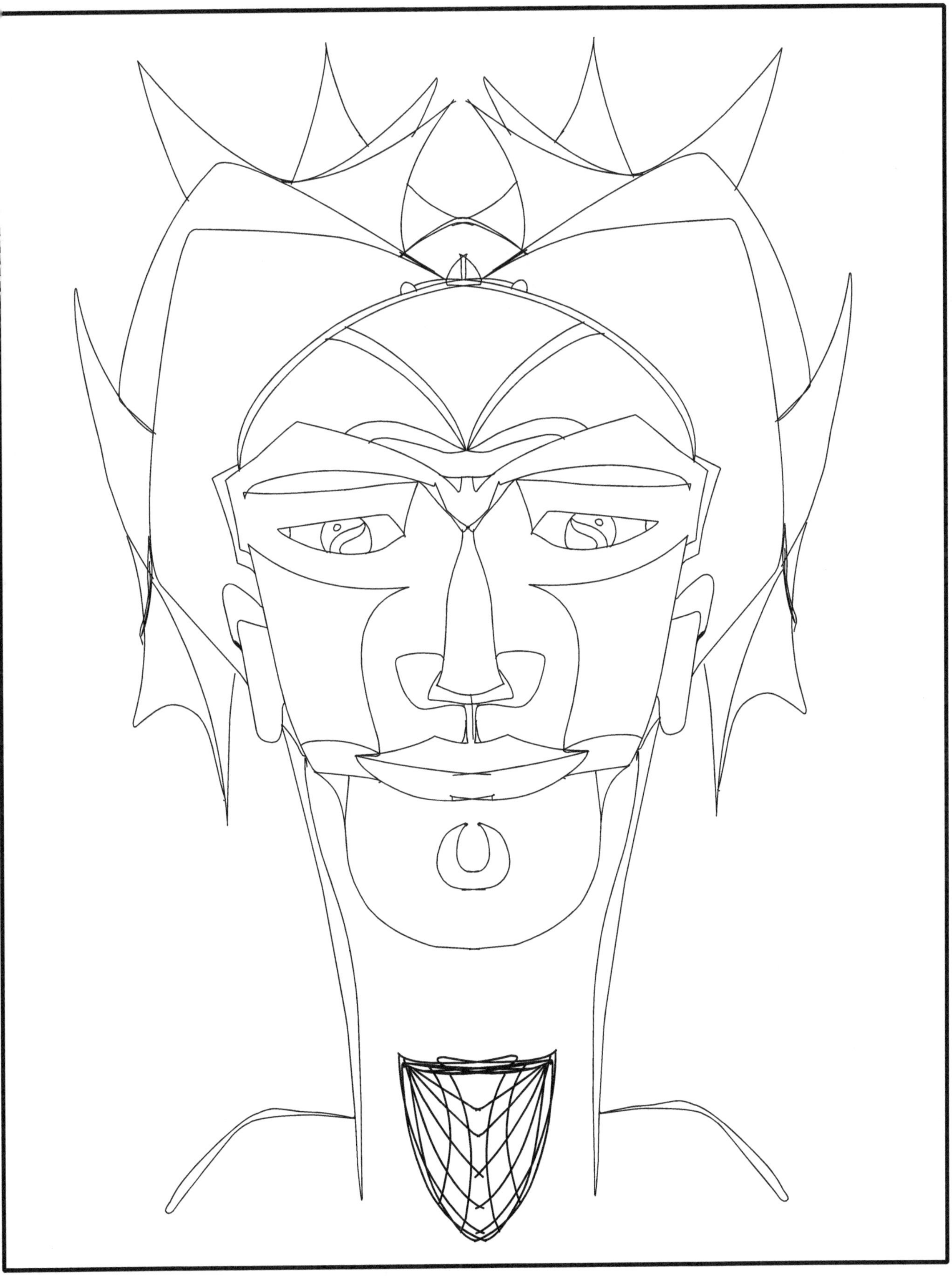

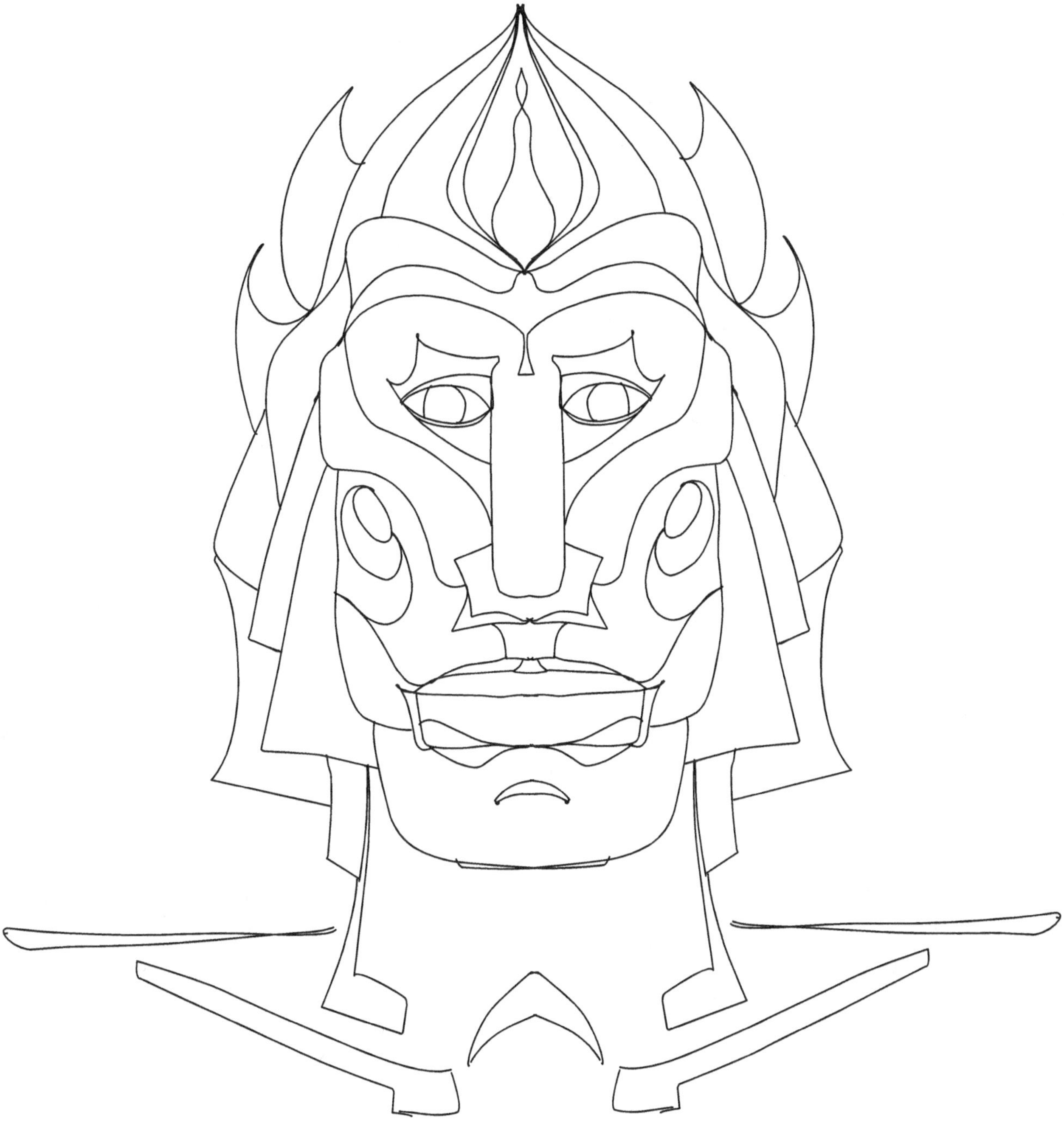

www.ingramcontent.com/pod-product-compliance
Lightning Source LLC
Chambersburg PA
CBHW082119220526
45472CB00009B/2243
* 9 7 9 8 6 8 2 2 4 4 3 3 1 *